AAC Visualized

A Visual Guide to Augmentative and Alternative Communication

Acknowledgments

The support and expertise of our collaborators has made *AAC Visualized* into a book we are truly proud of. Most notably, Michelle Austin has played a huge role in the development of this book, and we are beyond grateful that she has shared her knowledge and time with us. We would also like to recognize Tamar Bedoyan for her ongoing support, late night edits, and overall encouragement. *AAC Visualized* would not portray the feeling that it has without our incredibly talented illustrator, Saliha Caliskan, who has captured the emotions and essence of AAC users and their supporters so beautifully. We are so thankful for those who consulted with us, sharing their professional expertise and personal experiences: SLPs, BCBAs, advocates for the Deaf community, AAC users, parents of AAC users, AAC specialists, and Autistic self-advocates. Thank you specifically to Jacqui Wunderlich, Tiffany Joseph, and Laura Hayes. We'd also like to thank our dedicated supervisees who contributed to the research found throughout this book as well as the recommended resources: Cassandra Lindquist, Julia Bernasconi, Julianne Saad, and Amanda Kaylor. Lastly, we are incredibly grateful for the ongoing love and support of our friends and family. Thank you.

First published 2022

AAC Visualized is a product of Studio van Diepen LLC

Written by:
Morgan van Diepen, M.Ed., BCBA & Janna Bedoyan, M.Ed., NBCT

Foreword by:
Michelle Austin, M.A., CCC-SLP

Design and Art Direction by:
Boudewijn van Diepen

Illustrations by:
Saliha Caliskan

Edited by:
Rose M. Reynolds

www.ABAVisualized.com
info@ABAVisualized.com

www.StudiovanDiepen.com
mail@StudiovanDiepen.com

ISBN: 979-8-218-07872-0

Printed by Lightning Source in a sustainable way

Contents

Foreword

As I read this wonderful book on Augmentative and Alternative Communication (AAC), I thought back to when I first started supporting individuals with complex communication needs. Most of us take communication for granted. Think about your day; what have you communicated today? How have you communicated it? What would it be like if you were not understood by the people you were communicating with? What if you only had a few words you could say? What if those words were limited to just getting your needs met? Would that be enough for you?

Communication is at the heart of everything we do. Without communication, we are compromised in our ability to participate in life and may be discounted in our abilities. I have been blessed to be a part of many individuals' AAC teams and have kept my connections with AAC users and their families over the years. These connections have taught me so much about addressing communication that makes a life difference.

As a Speech Language Pathologist with over 30 years of specializing in AAC, the way we view and teach AAC has had many shifts. I have heard the frustration within families in not knowing where to go and how to support their loved one's communication. This led to my decision to address implementation differently. Through this decision, I created several AAC academies and collaborated with professionals to develop an online AAC social group called AAC Explorers: an AAC language-enriched environment focusing on AAC as a fully robust language, the importance of social connections, and supporting every member of the individual's AAC communication team.

It was in this type of environment that I first met Janna Bedoyan. I can remember her excitement as she created an AAC language environment. She would call it her AAC immersion classroom, and it truly was! She looked at every activity within her environment as a place where language happens, including AAC language! I was inspired by her excitement at watching her students' communication improve through the use of AAC as their communication system. The understanding of AAC implementation as a team approach has been further enhanced by Morgan van Diepen who brings another valued perspective to the implementation team. Together they look at building language through naturalistic approaches using a variety of applied behavioral techniques.

Working together, Janna and Morgan have helped many AAC teams by promoting collaboration and consultation with all professionals and parents. *AAC Visualized* presents AAC in a way that supports seeing AAC as a new language and, as such, discusses how we speak in this new language. They present practical solutions to building AAC implementation in every environment. Thus, building connections for everyone to see that we all have a role in teaching language. They provide an understanding of what AAC is and how great things will happen when we work together. I am excited for your journey to begin with *AAC Visualized*!

Michelle Austin, M.A., CCC-SLP
Speech Language Pathologist
Augmentative Alternative Communication Specialist
Assistive Technology Specialist

Note From the Authors

Everyone should have a voice. As advocates for people with disabilities and their families, we have seen firsthand how AAC can truly change someone's life. Having a way to communicate is the most powerful gift that you can give someone. While there are many knowledgeable experts within this field, our particular aim is to provide this information in an approachable, accessible, and relatable way so that the use of Augmentative and Alternative Communication (AAC) is more readily available and accepted by all. There are many myths and misconceptions about AAC, such as if you choose AAC, you give up on vocal speech. While this has been proven time and time again not to be accurate, myths like this are a barrier for individuals who could benefit from AAC. With this book, we hope to shine a light on how AAC can help someone truly be and express themselves.

Our hope is to empower families, teachers, and service providers to feel better prepared to work together seamlessly for the benefit of the AAC user. Unfortunately, even when each person has the best intentions, if the team is not collaborative, it is a disservice to the AAC user. For example, research has shown that when ABA (Applied Behavior Analysis) providers, including BCBAs (Board Certified Behavior Analysts), and SLPs (Speech Language Pathologists) have differing recommendations and use differing terms, it leaves the families and teachers feeling overwhelmed and confused. We intend to close the gap between these fields of expertise to impact those who truly need it: the AAC user and their family. In *AAC Visualized*, we have done this through the power of using visuals to teach essential AAC skills and concepts.

In holding true to our book's mission, we have tried to embody the importance of collaboration through consulting with many experts in creating this book. While there may seem to be glaring differences across fields, we have the same goal of building independence in communication for our learners. An example of this is when we (a teacher and a BCBA) were consulting with Michelle Austin (an SLP) on the protocol for responding to "missed opportunities" for communication, meaning the learner did not respond to a social opportunity or they engaged in challenging behaviors. We initially thought that our methodologies were so different, but through respectful conversations (and a lot of visual sketches!), we found that they were aligned. There is so much overlap between these fields, not only in theory but also in application. While the text of this book is intentionally written to be approachable for those new to AAC, we have highlighted the ABA and SLP technical concepts throughout the book (see Supporting Communication visual on page 88. for the end result of 8+ hours of collaboration!).

We recognize that this level of in-depth collaboration is not always feasible. That is why we have created a collection of Templates & Tools to highlight everyone's roles and responsibilities for easy and ongoing collaboration. AAC is a team effort!

By reading this book, you are already acting as an AAC advocate and supporter. Our goal is to spread AAC knowledge, helping you feel comfortable, confident, and inspired to support your AAC user.

Morgan van Diepen, M.Ed., BCBA

Janna Bedoyan, M.Ed., NBCT

Boudewijn van Diepen

About the Authors

Morgan van Diepen

Morgan is a Board Certified Behavior Analyst (BCBA) and Autism Specialist with over 15 years of working experience in the field of ABA. Through her international experience working with families and schools, Morgan's passion for disseminating behavior strategies in an engaging and approachable way expanded. She has presented at several national conferences and continues to act as an advocate for accessible behavioral expertise for families and teachers.

Janna Bedoyan

Janna is an Autism Early Childhood Education Teacher with over 10 years of experience in the classroom. She is a National Board Certified Teacher (NBCT) and Augmentative and Alternative Communication Specialist. She is deeply passionate about AAC, as she has spent much of her life helping children and their families find ways to communicate together. Janna loves nothing more than seeing the light in a child's eyes when they are able to communicate for the first time! AAC is her love language!

Boudewijn van Diepen

Boudewijn is an award-winning infographic designer who approaches every project from a conceptual and original perspective. His ability to effectively shape complex information into an understandable and aesthetically attractive visual is evidenced through his more than 10 years of diverse experience ranging from projects for government agencies to start-up nonprofit organizations. Boudewijn loves to use his creativity to make the world a more approachable place.

Our Mission

Our mission with *AAC Visualized* is to normalize the use of AAC, advocate for more acceptance and access to AAC, and empower families through collaboration and education.

Normalize

- Expand the acceptance of all forms of communication.
- Promote a mindset that one's abilities are not a determinant of their worth, value, and rights.
- Model inclusivity so that people feel accepted and welcome.

Advocate

- Celebrate neurodivergence by seeing the use of AAC not as something that needs to be fixed but instead as a part of someone.
- Create equity through AAC accessibility so that everyone has the same opportunities to thrive by expressing themselves.
- Remove barriers so that all people, regardless of ability, can communicate with those around them to the fullest extent possible.

Empower

- Encourage a collaborative effort to support AAC users.
- Close the gap between expert fields to create more successful and long-lasting impacts.
- Educate families to help them effectively advocate for their child's needs.

All About AAC

An Introduction to AAC

What is AAC?

Did you know that you use AAC every day and probably don't even realize it? When you are texting with your friend, sending an email to your coworker, writing a handwritten note, using gestures like a thumbs up or shrugging your shoulders, using facial expressions like smiling or rolling your eyes, it is all considered AAC. Augmentative & Alternative Communication (AAC) simply means any form of communication other than vocal speech. When you use an emoji or gif in response to a text message—you guessed it—that's also a form of AAC! To take it one step further: do you have predictive text on your phone? Or spell checker in a Word document? These are both examples of Assistive Technology (AT) that you use very often. AAC is Assistive Technology for communication. Most AAC systems have these features as well.

Imagine coming home from a long day at work: you are finally trying to relax on the couch, and your phone goes off; that immediate dread sets in like, "Oh, who's calling me now?!" You glance over at your phone to see who it is. You have a split second to decide if you will pick it up or let it go to voicemail and hope they text you after they hang up. Luckily, they do send you a text message, and you can respond to it instead of having a full-blown conversation on the phone. So even though you could speak to them, you can choose your response form: vocal, text message, emoji, or no response. This is exactly the same for an AAC user. When we force an AAC user to use one form of communication over another, that can be very stressful and almost traumatic. Instead, we should promote "multimodal communication," meaning that we accept any form of communication. This starts with realizing that, as adults, we use many different forms of communication throughout our day. We can check in with ourselves, the situation, and our communication partner and decide how and when we want to respond. An AAC user has this same right. And just like when you are tired or stressed, you revert to the easiest response mode for yourself, so do AAC users. That is why it is essential to accept all forms of communication from AAC users, especially when they are first learning how to use their communication system.

A new AAC user whose previous mode of communication was gestures may revert to gestures in a moment of frustration or to have the quickest response time. Another example is if you speak two or more languages, and in a moment of excitement or anger, you start speaking your native language without even realizing it! This is because that is the language you think in and process in. That is your fastest communication mode. The hope is that AAC users will become fluent in their AAC language and have the freedom to communicate in the way they want to at a given moment.

Let's break down the acronym. We already know that AAC stands for Augmentative and Alternative Communication, but what do augmentative and alternative actually mean? They are slightly different.

Augmentative means to add to or support someone's speech. Some AAC users have speech and may talk to communicate. They may need to use an AAC system if their speech is not clear to help them express the thoughts in their mind that they are having a hard time verbalizing. Others may have difficulty with language, such as finding the right words at the moment, and can gain support from the visuals to augment their communication. Think about when you are having a "tip of the tongue" moment, and you try to describe the word but still can't figure out the exact word you are looking for. It will annoy you if you can't remember it, so you pull out your phone to try to google it or look for a picture of what you are describing. That is how an AAC user also uses AAC.

The second "A" in AAC stands for alternative. Alternative communication is used instead of the individual's speech. Alternative communication helps to support individuals who are not using vocal speech or have limited vocal skills. Often, a non-speaking person will have many thoughts they wish to communicate but may not have the ability to do so with their current communication abilities. AAC can provide a way for them to express themselves. While this is true across all ages, it is especially important for young children who are still learning to communicate. AAC can help them learn how to communicate effectively, reduce challenging behaviors, and may even help them develop speech skills down the road. Using sign language is a form of alternative communication and it's not exclusively used by deaf individuals. Even if you are hearing and speaking, you are welcome to learn and use signs to better communicate with the deaf and hard of hearing community around you!

Communication is a two-way street. Not only does AAC improve communication, research shows that it also reduces frustration for AAC users and their communication partners. When messages cannot be accurately conveyed, it can reduce the motivation to communicate, ultimately hiding an AAC user's voice. However, with AAC, everyone can be on the same page and better understand each other. This can help build stronger relationships and improve communication overall.

AAC can be used by anyone who struggles with vocal communication. There are people who use AAC as an augmentative system, there are people who use it as an alternative system, and for some people, it depends on the day or the situation. No matter the reasons for using AAC, the benefits are the same! Communication!!

A common question we hear is something like, "My child has eight words and can speak, so why does he need a communication device to speak for him?" For one second, put yourself in that child's shoes and imagine you could only use eight words all day, every day! These words might be something like: cookie, juice, more, cracker, want, gummy bear, and ball. Could you get through your entire workday with just these eight words? Probably not. Imagine how frustrated and irritated your coworkers would be if the only responses you could give them were, "I want juice" or "More ball." Your boss recognizes your frustration and coworkers' irritations, so he decides to get you a brand-new laptop. Now you can type any word you need to get your job done and communicate with your team more effectively. That is the same sentiment as giving someone a communication system or device. They now have access to hundreds of words they can use throughout their day to express themselves more fully and effectively. So, even though someone can speak a few words or use several signs, that is not enough language to fully communicate throughout one's lifetime.

Why is AAC effective?

Recent research has found that AAC devices are effective at helping people learn language. Researchers have suggested that this is because the device gives an immediate voice output. This voice output can help them understand how symbols and spoken sounds are linked together, which can help improve conversational skills and promote quicker communication independence. Further, research also suggests that this immediate voice output can be rewarding for the AAC user to hear, meaning they are motivated to continue using it. This is important to consider when seeing your AAC user "talk to themselves" or "stimming" with their device. Instead of viewing this as "nonfunctional communication," meaning there is no communication partner, try seeing it as the AAC user exploring their AAC language on their own! A comparison is when neurotypical children are babbling. They do this throughout the day and sometimes even when alone! Experimenting with sounds and words is part of typical language development. (See page 124 for more on stimming with AAC).

AAC is a tool that enables better communication for both the AAC user and their communication partner. The visual component of AAC adds an extra layer of communication, often resulting in a clearer message. There is substantial research on the benefits of visuals. They enable people to understand meanings more quickly and more accurately, thus often relieving anxiety around unclear situations. Whether the AAC user is using a core board, AAC device, or signing, these can all be used as visual forms of communication!

Where to start?

There are so many questions and considerations that it can feel overwhelming, and you may not know where to start. If you are brand new to AAC, we recommend paying particular attention to our four tips in the "Introducing AAC" chapter and "Discussing AAC Myths" on page 44.

Sometimes we encounter the "wait and see" approach. But imagine you find out that your child is d/Deaf or hard of hearing or has low vision at their one-year check-up. You would immediately find an audiologist or eye doctor to see if a hearing aid or eyeglasses would be beneficial. Some of our favorite videos on social media are where toddlers get their hearing aids and can hear their mother's voice for the first time. You can see the light that floods their eyes when they hear their mother say, "I love you." This is truly an unparalleled moment. But in contrast, sometimes, when there is a recommendation for an AAC device, there is so much fear and sometimes push back, or the "let's wait and see" approach. AAC is adding a piece of technology to improve someone's life. Just like adding hearing aids so that someone can hear or glasses so that someone can see. Adding AAC to someone's life so that they can "speak" is the same. One of our goals from this book is to normalize AAC so that more individuals can access effective communication sooner.

If you think your learner could benefit from AAC or a trusted friend or professional has recommended this to you, the first step is to get an AAC Assessment. We have outlined the different routes to getting this assessment on page 50. The initial assessment can take some time, so request this right away if you think your child, student, or family member needs an AAC system. You are now their AAC advocate!

In the meantime, we recommend starting to teach AAC with a core board. This visual includes symbols of commonly used words that have a lot of versatility in daily life, called "core words" (read more about this on page 60). We have created a core board that you can copy and print to use while you wait for your individualized recommendations following the completion of the AAC assessment (page 140). All of the strategies for introducing and expanding AAC found within this book can be used with any form of AAC, including this printed core board or an AAC device.

Finally, start building your AAC team! Your team may include your learner's Speech Language Pathologist (SLP), their teachers, family members, Board Certified Behavior Analysts (BCBAs), other ABA practitioners, and other relevant service providers. This team will be there to support you even after the AAC assessment is complete and you are ready to implement AAC collaboratively!

Who can use AAC?

Everyone uses some AAC for communication (anytime we text, for example), and anyone whose needs are not met by speech alone can benefit from additional AAC support. We cannot always tell if someone would benefit from or uses an AAC support just by looking at them or knowing their diagnosis. Also, suppose a person can speak some of the time. In that case, they may still need an AAC device to help them communicate more effectively or easily. An AAC device gives them more words and clear language to communicate better and with more people than before or without the device.

Some people who use AAC are non-speaking. There are so many different reasons why someone is not able to speak. They may have a developmental disability or an acquired disorder that affects their ability to talk. Some people's speech deteriorates over time because of a medical condition. They may have lost the ability to speak because of stress, anxiety, trauma, or even a medical emergency like a stroke or traumatic brain injury. This may be temporary or lifelong. No matter the reason or disability, AAC can be used to improve the quality of someone's life.

There are no age limits on AAC. Anyone can use it! Think about someone who has recently had a stroke or a traumatic brain injury who may have temporarily lost the ability to speak—they could use AAC. Or an older woman with dementia who has difficulty pulling up words in her brain—AAC could benefit her! Or what about baby signs—there are hundreds of books and research on the benefits of using baby signs, which is also a form of AAC. If baby signs are normalized, so should the use of all forms of AAC. It's never too late or too early to start AAC. From infants to the elderly, AAC is for everyone!

The Autistic community

While there are many reasons why someone may use AAC, a significant number of AAC users are autistic. As of the date of publication, the prevalence of autism is 1 in 44 individuals. It is estimated that about 25% of this population are nonvocal or "minimally verbal," defined as using fewer than 30 functional vocal words or unable to use speech alone to communicate. It's important to remember that although someone is not communicating vocally, this does not mean that they cannot understand or cannot learn. With the growing access to autism support services for clients & families, AAC is a powerful tool for many autisitic individuals. It can help bridge the gap between their inner thoughts and the outside world and can help them develop stronger bonds with others, allowing them to feel more included in the world around them. AAC has truly changed the lives of many autistic people for the better.

We know that many of our autistic learners do well with visual supports. It is important to understand that AAC devices work by presenting the user with a visual representation of the words they wish to communicate to their communication partner. The user can then select the appropriate word or phrase from the AAC device to communicate their message. For many autistic individuals, this visual representation of language makes it easier to express themselves compared to spoken language.

In addition, AAC devices can also help reduce frustration, increase confidence, and improve social skills. With an AAC device, individuals no longer have to rely on others to interpret their words and intentions; they can communicate directly, which often leads to improved social interactions.

The Deaf community

One of the oldest forms of AAC is one you may not expect—signed languages. There are hundreds of different signed languages worldwide, and various sign languages have existed for thousands of years, not just used by d/Deaf people (note: the writing of "d/Deaf" is intended to be inclusive of those who identify as being within the cultural Deaf community as those who don't). In the Ottoman empire, deaf servants were favored by the Sultan and highly sought out by courtiers to tutor their children in learning to sign. A number of indigenous North American nations used "Plains Indian Sign Language" not only within their own people to pass on cultural heritage but to communicate across different spoken languages with other indigenous nations. Plains Indian Sign Language is still used today. Most recently, from the 18th century until the 20th century, Martha's Vineyard Sign Language was utilized by most islanders, regardless of their hearing level on the small Massachusetts island. Throughout history and into the present, signed languages have brought people together and allowed diverse groups to communicate and flourish.

One of the things that makes American Sign Language (ASL) so special is its focus on accessibility and inclusion. The Deaf community has always been at the forefront of the fight for accessibility rights, and ASL is one of the ways in which they have been able to do this. By making their language available to everyone, they have been able to break down barriers and connect with people from all walks of life. This inclusive approach has led to a resurgence in interest in ASL in recent years, as more and more people are looking for ways to connect with the Deaf community and learn about their culture and history.

As of this publication date, around one million individuals in the United States use American Sign Language (ASL) as their primary language and method of communication. It's important to note that ASL is just as rich and complete a language as any spoken language—babies given access to ASL follow the same milestones as spoken languages, babbling on their hands and then beginning to sign in one or two-word sentences. d/Deaf and hard of hearing people often use a wide variety of AAC methods to communicate on a daily basis, such as writing back and forth, texting, pointing, using apps to communicate, and so much more. ASL is deeply rooted in the Deaf community, so it is important to seek out Deaf teachers when learning. But ASL is ultimately a language built on the values of accessibility and connection—and so everyone is welcome to use it, no matter how much or how little you hear. Welcome to the Deaf community. We're glad to have you.

Written in collaboration with Jacqueline Wunderlich, M.A., BCBA, LBA
Signs of Communication, LLC

AAC Users

We all use AAC! We use gestures, facial expressions, and electronic communication to communicate more easily or to make our communication more clear. For some, AAC is their primary form of communication. Within this population, they may be speaking or non-speaking. Furthermore, AAC use could be temporary or long-term. What is important is that they have a voice, whatever mode it may be! In the below bubbles, we have identified reasons why someone may be an AAC user or why AAC could benefit them.

Reasons why someone may benefit from AAC

Apraxia & dyspraxia

Cerebral palsy

Speech Language Impairment (SLI)

Stroke

Developmental delays

Cognitive impairments

d/Deaf & hard of hearing

Autism Spectrum Disorders (ASDs)

Degenerative diseases

Physical disabilities

Traumatic Brain Injury (TBI)

AAC Supporters

AAC supporters are a crucial part of an AAC user's life! They provide the encouragement and motivation AAC users need to keep communication alive. AAC supporters do not speak for the AAC user but rather help them to find their own voice. They offer guidance and support, but ultimately, AAC users are in control of their communication. AAC supporters play an important role in making sure that AAC users have the opportunity to be heard. AAC supporters are essential members of the AAC user's life and contribute to their well-being, making a tremendous difference in the lives of AAC users.

Those who can support AAC users

Daycare staff

Speech Language Pathologists (SLPs)

Family & friends

Occupational Therapists (OTs)

Other service providers

Teachers

Paraprofessionals

Applied Behavior Analysis (ABA) providers

Interveners

Medical staff

Everyone!

Babysitters

Parents/ caregivers

Employer/ colleagues

AAC supporters can play a vital role in providing AAC users with the consistent support they need to communicate effectively. AAC supporters can help AAC users to select and use AAC strategies, provide modeling and practice opportunities, and offer emotional support. In addition, AAC supporters can help to ensure that AAC strategies are used in a way that is respectful of the AAC user's wishes and preferences. Every AAC user deserves the opportunity to have a nurturing AAC supporter who can help them to communicate their thoughts and feelings effectively.

AAC supporters are a vital part of the team when it comes to supporting someone's right to communicate. By being an advocate, cheerleader, and patient guide, you can help AAC user's navigate the world of communication—a world that is often filled with barriers and misunderstanding.

AAC users often face the challenge of inconsistent support. This means that they may only be heard in some places, sometimes. AAC users would benefit greatly from a plan to select and train one or more people to be their AAC supporters. For school-aged children, most AAC users may require an assigned facilitator who has the authority to make changes for the AAC user with their system. With specific training, a teacher or paraprofessional would be a great person to be the AAC facilitator for the AAC user at school. If the AAC user is an adult, an ideal choice would be a partner/spouse or disability support staff. In the workplace, an AAC facilitator is also a great idea. This could be someone with intuition and knowledge, prepared to make adjustments on behalf of individuals' needs when necessary—such as adding accommodations to work-related tasks. In addition, this AAC facilitator should have enough authority and knowledge on how best to accommodate those with disabilities to enjoy an equitable education or work experience.

Tips for AAC supporters

- Acknowledge all communication attempts
- Keep it fun!
- Model more
- Keep it consistent
- Collaborate as a team

Types of AAC

When it comes to AAC, there are two main types: unaided and aided. Unaided AAC relies on the body to communicate, while aided AAC uses external tools. You can use high-tech tools, like a Speech Generating Device (SGD), also known as an "AAC device," or low-tech tools, like a communication book or core board. This technology is expanding rapidly, giving more and more access to effective communication for AAC users. One communication system is not better than another; it is all individualized to best fit the AAC user. The SLP in your collaborative team will help you identify the best fit and most preferred system for your AAC user.

Types of AAC

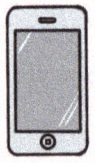
Texting

Typing/emails

Single message voice output

Sign language

Speech Generating Device (SGD)

Facial expressions

Eye gaze

Picture Communication Exchange System (PECS)

Speech Generating Device (SGD) with a key guard

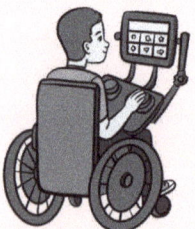
Alternative access two-step scanning

Single switch voice output

Understanding Speech vs. Language

Speech and language are often considered the same since they are combined in the title for the service provider who supports this need: Speech and Language Pathologist. However, speech and language are very different and require different therapy approaches. Speech is the production of sounds, and language is the combination of words. When it comes to AAC, you can work on both!

A speech disorder could look like not producing the correct sounds, stuttering, nasal or hoarse voice, or articulation errors. Receptive Language Disorder is having a hard time understanding language or interpreting meanings. Expressive Language Disorder is difficulty expressing ideas, thoughts, and feelings.

Speech

Language

Articulation
wabbit vs.
rabbit

Expressive
combining words
to communicate a
message

Fluency
smoothness
and rhythm
(also referred
to as stuttering)

Receptive
comprehension &
understanding of
language

Voice
loud, soft,
high, low

Pragmatics
unspoken rules of
communication in social
situation

Understanding AAC as a Visual Language

One specific benefit of symbol-based AAC is that it makes language visual! When we speak words aloud, once they escape our lips, they are gone forever. However, with AAC, language becomes much more permanent and lasts longer because AAC is a visual language. Every word is paired with an icon, symbol, picture, or word. This makes language last longer because we can see it instead of only hearing it. It also makes language that can be very abstract much more concrete for both the AAC user and their communication partner.

Let's try something! What do you think the symbol below means?

Not sure? What if we told you it is pronounced "ring-oh"? Now can you guess what the symbol means?

Now turn to the next page (bottom right). With the additional visual, you now understand! That is the power of having a visual language. Understanding happens faster when multiple elements (such as sound, visual, text) are presented simultaneously. In this example, the Japanese character, the pronunciation, and the visual all help to teach the meaning (ABA terminology: stimulus class concept formation).

Let's try another one!

Out of the symbols below, which one do you think represents "like"? What about "want"? And "this"?

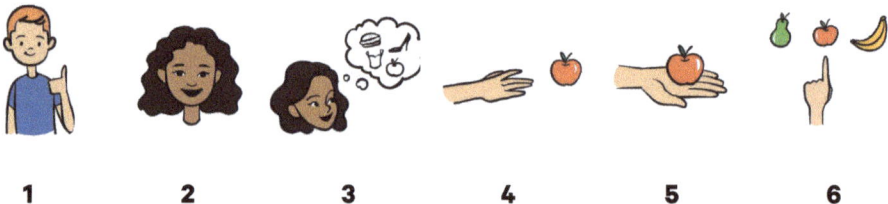

| 1 | 2 | 3 | 4 | 5 | 6 |

Turn to the next page to check your answers. Not so easy, right? Just having a visual is sometimes not enough even for commonly understood words. Look at our core board on page 140. You are able to understand the symbols because we have paired the word with them. For early literacy learners, you will have to *teach* the concept of the symbols. You can do this through modeling, which you will learn how to do in our Introducing AAC chapter!

AAC is a tool that enables better communication for both the AAC user and their communication partner. The visual component of AAC adds an extra layer of communication, often resulting in a clearer message. For example, imagine you just landed in a foreign country. You need to buy a train ticket, but you do not speak or read the language. Imagine feeling relieved when you see a train illustration with an arrow. This example gives insight into how visuals can quickly convey a lot of meaning.

It's not just icons and symbols! Seeing someone's facial expressions as they are telling you a story affects your understanding of the story. This is visual! It's the same for using emojis in your texts to clarify your tone further. For d/Deaf individuals, in addition to their signs being visual communication, their exaggerated facial expressions and body movements also convey a more complete and clear message.

While AAC is a visual language, communicating with visuals benefits more than just AAC users. As a teacher, you can use visuals to help your students learn new skills, understand expectations more clearly, and improve self-management skills. By incorporating AAC into vocal instructions, teachers can create a more inclusive classroom, accommodating all students' needs.

Research indicates that visuals help by

- Allowing students to focus on key words and concepts
- Making abstract concepts more visually concrete
- Encouraging students to more easily express their thoughts
- Reducing anxiety and frustration
- Serving as a tool to assist with communication
- Increasing comprehension
- Decreasing challenging behaviors

Understanding Analytic Language Processing

What is analytic language processing?

Analytic language processing is a natural language development style in which a child learns that individual words each carry a particular meaning—for example, first learning to label "dog" when shown a four-legged animal that barks. Over time, the child learns to combine words with phrases and then into sentences. For example, "dog" → "dog sleeping" → "the cute dog is sleeping."

How do I know if my child is an analytic language processor?

Their early language may involve first using single words and then combining familiar words to make two to three-word phrases. In addition, their language is often generalized to similar objects and activities across the day, meaning they use words and phrases in different, accurate contexts.

How does analytic language processing relate to AAC?

Most robust AAC language software has been created based on analytic language development, so analytic language processors may more naturally take on the use of the AAC system. AAC should be considered a tool for any analytic language processor showing signs of communication breakdowns and frustration or having difficulty generating flexible, spontaneous language.

Written in collaboration with Laura Hayes, M.S., CCC-SLP
AAC Innovations

Understanding Gestalt Language Processing

What is gestalt language processing?

Gestalt language processing is another natural language development style in which a child learns language through intonation and longer "chunks" and units of language that could be words, phrases, and sentences, known as gestalts. For example, first learning to label "dog" as "it's a dog." Over time, these gestalts can be broken down and then learned to be recombined to support flexible language. For example, "it's a dog" and "it's sleeping" → "dog" and "sleeping" → "the dog is sleeping."

How do I know if my child is a gestalt language processor?

Gestalt language processors often show delayed or immediate echolalia (repeating back entire words/phrases/sentences they hear). These learners may have long strings of speech that are not easily understood by others. They often use rich intonation when communicating, as shown by changing their rhythm and tone. Also, their language may be "stuck" to certain contexts/situations and not easily generalized across contexts.

How does gestalt language processing relate to AAC?

As AAC organization is based on analytic language development, gestalt language processors in the early stages of language development may need customizations of scripts/gestalts that the child will find valuable and important (ask your SLP for help!). Exposure to audio or video clips with rich and original intonation may be helpful. For these types of processors, your SLP or AAC specialist can help make individualized choices, as there is not one specific system designed for AAC users who are gestalt language processors (yet!).

Answers from previous page

Activity 1

林檎

"ring-oh"

Activity 2

2, 3, 6

Understanding the Importance of Collaboration

People in the AAC user's life want to help the AAC user build communication skills. Sometimes, they each have different ideas about how to do that. When this happens, it can be confusing for the family and the AAC user. Research has shown that when there are discrepancies between SLPs' and ABA providers' recommendations, it can be a hindrance to the AAC user's progress. Additionally, each field has their own set of jargon. These different terms can be a significant source of confusion for the family and a barrier to collaboration. This happens because the family and AAC user do not know how to integrate the different recommendations into their lives. Even if each practitioner uses evidence-based practices from within their field, if there is no collaboration, the AAC user may not make as much progress. In the illustration below, you can see an unfortunate common occurence. Although each AAC supporter is focusing on teaching an effective AAC system, because they're not aligned, the AAC user and family are left feeling confused.

Individual approach

SLP

Teacher

Paraprofessional

ABA provider

Occupational Therapist (OT)

When all AAC supporters come together, there can be truly meaningful progress. People from various backgrounds make up the AAC team (see page 26 for AAC supporters). The AAC learner is an important member of the team and should participate as much as possible. Everyone who interacts with the AAC learner can contribute to the success of AAC. This is because communication occurs all the time in almost every situation. Research shows that collaboration can lead to faster skill development and longer-lasting results, and AAC users prefer it!

Use our Collaboration Plan (page 142) to help promote a collaborative approach to supporting your AAC user. As a team, determine the communication mode, communication goals, and a cohesive plan for teaching these skills. Set timelines so that everyone knows when these goals need to be accomplished. When the team is on board with the goals and direction, the chances of success are much greater.

Collaborative approach

SLP

Teacher

Paraprofessional

ABA provider

Occupational Therapist (OT)

SLP's role

The Speech Language Pathologist (SLP) is responsible for conducting AAC assessments, teaching AAC implementation, consulting, and coaching other team members. AAC assessments involve determining the appropriate access for the AAC user, type of AAC system, the number and size of locations/icons, and how the language is organized. Upon completion of the AAC assessment, a list of features is developed and matched to a specific language or communication system. This helps the team determine what will be most appropriate for the AAC user. During a trial period, the AAC user can try out different communication systems to find which one meets their current and future communication needs and preferences. Throughout the AAC assessment and trials, the AAC team must presume potential, which is the belief that an individual has the ability and potential to do or learn to do something that they have not done before.

It is important to note that the AAC assessment process is an ongoing process. The AAC user's communication, needs, and goals will continuously change as the AAC user develops more communication skills. The SLP will continue to assess and determine if the AAC system is appropriate, whether it is still meeting the AAC user's needs, has room for more language to grow, or needs to be modified to meet the AAC user's current level of communication. Presuming potential is an essential guiding belief in working with AAC users.

As part of an IEP (Individualized Education Program) team, the SLP will create goals and objectives and may provide initial and ongoing training to teachers, families, and other IEP team members. The SLP will develop and support an AAC implementation plan as a team member. The AAC implementation plan helps the team work together to maximize the AAC user's communication growth in multiple environments, focusing on the AAC Competencies (Operational Competence, Functional/Social Competence, Linguistic Competence, Strategic Competence, and Emotional Competence—see page 146 for more on AAC competencies). SLPs can share their expertise to ensure that goals are age and developmentally appropriate based on language development and language learning. An SLP is the go-to person to ensure that all decisions around AAC and language are the best fit for the user!

Written in collaboration with Michelle Austin, M.A., CCC-SLP

Family's role

Parent involvement is vital to provide a more personalized assessment and support plan because they are the expert on their child and family. The family's role in this process is crucial because they can offer input into the specific communication needs of their child. Families help provide information about any concerns or limitations that may arise during usage at home or in the community. They participate by sharing specific vocabulary related to their child's preferences, interests, and culture. They are part of the IEP team and attend meetings, review IEP goals/objectives, and advocate for their child. Family roles are crucial to carrying AAC over and into the home and the community, as communication happens all the time! Service providers should take extra steps to ensure families actively participate in AAC decisions and trainings. Sometimes, the family may need to take a leading role as an AAC advocate for their child. It helps to have an AAC community, even if it's an online community of other families with AAC users who can relate to your experience. We have put some recommendations for resources in the Tools & Templates section of this book. The family's role is the most essential of all AAC supporters. Research shows that families often learn the communication strategies taught by SLPs and ABA providers quickly and accurately!

Presume potential means that you believe that your child can learn how to communicate differently and with AAC. That you honor and validate what they are communicating. That you support the idea that AAC use happens everywhere: at school, at home, and in the community. Parents and caregivers are the most important team members, and successful AAC use hinges on parents and caregivers. Specifically, parents, caregivers, and other communication partners have the unique ability to create communication opportunities for their AAC user and increase responsiveness to communication attempts. Research shows that when parents are better at creating communication opportunities for their children, this results in greater child communication in initiations, communicative turns, and use of different language concepts.

As a parent of an AAC user, one of the most important jobs is to help our AAC users develop strong communication skills. Unfortunately, many nonvocal children are deprived of opportunities for communication and socialization because adults around them do not know how to communicate with them or that they are even capable of communication. However, by modeling AAC (introducing them to their AAC system by communicating with it yourself), we are giving our learners opportunities for communication and socialization that they would not have had otherwise. Modeling is one of the most important things we can do as parents of AAC users (you'll learn how to do this later in this book!). It helps close the time gap between AAC introduction and independence, exposes our children to their "language," and gives them opportunities for communication and socialization. So let's ensure that we are modeling to provide the most expeditious route to progress and independence!

3 ways you can help your child as an AAC supporter

1. Be their biggest cheerleader. Believe in your child and their ability to communicate. They may use a different method than you are used to, but that does not mean they cannot communicate effectively. Show your child that you believe in them and will support them in whatever method of communication they choose.
2. Be their advocate. Some people will not understand how your child communicates or why they use AAC instead of speech. Stand up for your child and explain how important communication is for them. Help others to see your child the way you do—as a competent individual with a lot to say!
3. Be patient and learn alongside them. Learning how to use and model AAC takes time and practice. Be patient with your child as they learn and make mistakes along the way. Remember that you are learning too! The more you know about AAC, the better equipped you will be to support your child in their communication journey.

Teacher's role

The teacher's role is first to understand the importance of modeling and then design the classroom to promote communication opportunities throughout the day. This is a shift from the common misconception that AAC should be practiced only during a particular time of the day, like snack time, or at a certain area, like the play area. Communication happens all day, every day! Therefore, setting up a classroom environment that supports and encourages AAC use starts with the teacher.

When working with students who use AAC, it is crucial to remember that they are just like any other student in your class. They have their own unique skills and abilities, and they deserve to be treated with respect and dignity. Presuming potential means believing that a person has the ability to do something, even if they have not yet proven it. This attitude is crucial because it can change how we interact with our students and the opportunities we give them. By presumption of potential in our students, we are setting them up for success inside and outside the classroom.

The teacher should also encourage other support staff to use AAC as much as possible, creating an accepting and supportive classroom. Support staff are often the communication partners of AAC users. As teachers model AAC for students, they are simultaneously modeling for their support staff. This is an added benefit to modeling! By incorporating the use of AAC within classroom norms and routines, the teacher is creating a classroom environment of AAC inclusion and AAC immersion. It may take some time to get "buy-in" from support staff, but as they see their students becoming more and more successful with using AAC, they will want to encourage that success and start to model AAC too! They may not be comfortable with technology or may think that it will stop or prevent a student from speaking or make them reliant on the AAC device instead of talking. The teacher's role is to find what barriers may be preventing a support member from embracing AAC in their classroom and teach, train, and celebrate support staff success with AAC.

Give support staff adequate time to observe your modeling. Research shows that using AAC within the classroom benefits not only the AAC user but other students who could use language support and visual support throughout their day. Teachers play a critical role in integrating AAC use into academic learning so that AAC users have more opportunities to thrive in their education. To help support teachers' use of AAC in the classroom, we have created two planning forms which can be found in the Templates & Tools chapter!

ABA provider's role

In Applied Behavior Analysis (ABA), practitioners create an individualized plan to support learners with essential skills, including independence in daily living, social and play skills, and communication skills. A significant overlap between ABA and SLP professionals is their shared expertise in supporting individuals with their communication needs. When considering where ABA providers fit into the AAC support team, it is essential to recognize their own strengths and limitations. Specifically, ABA providers have extensive knowledge of how communication is linked to challenging behaviors and can propose specific communication targets that may help reduce these behaviors (to learn more about ABA, check out our flagship book, *ABA Visualized!*). ABA providers can also create individualized goals based on an assessment of specific communication skills, including requesting ("manding"), labeling ("tacting"), copying ("echoics"), and conversation skills ("intraverbals"), and can make evidence-based recommendations of how to teach these skills. ABA providers also have expertise with data collection, making them an excellent choice for the role of analyzing the progress and effectiveness of the collaborative plan. ABA providers can then collaborate closely with SLPs, who have comprehensive training when it comes to language development and AAC acquistion.

When working with AAC users, especially early AAC learners, it is essential that we presume potential when choosing goals and teaching skills. In ABA, this may look like collaborating with SLPs to determine goals that best align with the AAC user's current strengths and stage of language development to ensure that we are not choosing goals that are too easy for them. Additionally, we must create opportunities for AAC users to show their communication strengths by providing access to robust language and moving beyond requests.

It's important for ABA providers also to be aware of their collaborative barriers. Research has shown that the technical jargon used by ABA providers can be "harsh" and "unmotivating" to other team members. It is recommended that ABA providers use approachable language when collaborating, as we have modeled throughout this book. Further, we recommend that ABA providers recognize the specific expertise that SLPs bring to the table by encouraging a collaborative approach to service recommendations related to communication skills. In many cases, the ABA team has the opportunity to develop strong relationships, rapport, and trust with the AAC user's family. This is a great opportunity for ABA providers to advocate for the creation of a collaborative communication plan, ensuring that their service goals align with the SLP's and those of the school team.

AAC user's role

The AAC user knows what they want to say. It's ultimately up to them to be creative in determining how to communicate at any given moment. They will have insight into which words are most meaningful, if they prefer symbols or spelling, and how easy or hard it is to express something. For example, learning disabilities may impact someone's success with using typing as AAC, and thus, they may prefer using gestures. Or motor difficulties may influence their preference for different AAC systems. Overall, the AAC user should be given opportunities to take the lead in their life and communication decisions.

As part of the AAC assessment process, AAC users are provided several systems or apps to trial. The team must look for signs of preference to help advocate for the best match for the AAC user. Once a system has been chosen, the AAC user's role doesn't stop there! For those that use AAC devices, they should have a choice in their voice output and accents. They know the mood and tone of how they want to communicate and can even choose accents based on this! For example, if they were engaging in pretend play with peers, they could adjust speech settings to a pirate voice or an older man's voice to enhance the silliness of the situation. They could also change the voice setting to emotive voices, like "sad voice," to express themselves more deeply. Although they may not initially know about all their device options, they always know what they want to say and how to say it.

Once an AAC user is proficient in customizing their own device (SLP terminology: operational contingencies), they should be given free access to do this, and their setting customizations should be seen as the gold standard—no one should change it. Brightness, volume, and color are all sensorial experiences for the AAC user. The AAC user understands their sensory experience and what they need at that moment. Once they know how to navigate their AAC device independently, they have to be completely trusted and believed that they know what's best for their communication. AAC users won't use their device if it's not their voice. Once AAC users are fully independent in using their AAC system, their role continues through self-determination and advocacy. They can choose which communication mode works better for them at the moment, tell others how they prefer to communicate, and decide if AAC is their primary language (remember, vocal speech is not always the end goal). A tip to promote self-advocacy is creating a card or a pre-programmed button that says something like, "This is my talking voice. This is how I speak, but you can speak back to me," or "Please type back to me so I can better understand you." Throughout the AAC user's life, they should be an active member of the collaborative team and have a say in decisions made in their best interests.

Written in collaboration with Tiffany Joseph, AAC user and advocate

Discussing AAC Myths

Introducing AAC means giving up on vocal speech

Some parents worry that if they give their child an AAC system, they will not learn to speak. In our experience, this is the most common myth and the most significant barrier to why families are hesitant to try AAC. However, research has shown that this is not usually the case. Often the opposite happens—the individual becomes more able to speak vocal words once they have an AAC system. For some, AAC can act as a bridge to vocal communication. According to research, 89% of participants who use AAC improve their speech skills. AAC is an important tool for individuals who struggle with speech, as it can reduce the psychological or emotional stress of being unable to communicate and ease the speech development process. In addition, research has shown that AAC has positive outcomes in terms of language development and literacy, as it supports self-expression in social and academic situations. Researchers believe AAC can enhance speech production because it offers AAC users a more immediate and consistent model, especially when AAC users use a speech-generating device. The addition of the visual component of AAC can truly enhance communication growth!

Bilingual families should choose only one language to use with the AAC user

There are many myths surrounding bilingualism and AAC. One common myth is that because AAC users struggle to learn one language, they will struggle to learn two. Research demonstrates that we need to reshape our views of early bilingualism. The research is clear: bilingual children can readily distinguish two languages and show no evidence of confusion. These findings have been consistent across studies of populations of neurotypical children, those with intellectual disabilities, Autism Spectrum Disorder (ASD), and Down syndrome. If AAC users blend or switch back and forth between languages, that's okay! We want to accept all forms of communication. You can even customize an AAC system to feel like a part of your home by adding things that reflect your culture, including foods, religion, and family traditions. A tip for AAC users who communicate in one language at school and another at home is to keep the icons in the same order and with the same visual symbol: just switch the language after school! Teachers can help by switching the device to the home language before the student leaves to go home. Most AAC systems are pre-loaded with many different languages and can be switched back and forth very quickly. This is a feature that the team will want to consider during the AAC assessment if assessing a bilingual individual or student.

AAC is only for nonvocal individuals

Another misconception is that only fully nonvocal individuals use AAC. As mentioned in our "Who can use AAC" introduction, we all use AAC every day. Some people may feel more comfortable using different communication modes in different situations. For example, someone who is d/Deaf and uses sign language and hearing aids may sometimes communicate with vocal language when speaking to hearing people even if sign is their primary communication, meaning most preferred and most comfortable. Think about individuals who have emerging vocal communication. This can be limiting when expressing thoughts, feelings, and opinions, so supplementing their communication with AAC allows for a much deeper social connection. In uncomfortable situations, an AAC user who typically speaks may prefer to use AAC. This may help navigate situations where clear communication is really needed. Maybe this is something that you relate to! Suppose you are working through something stressful or emotional. In that case, you may find it easier to write/journal your thoughts rather than vocally express them to someone. Just as at this moment, you are using a form of AAC (writing), we want to ensure that AAC users have the same access and rights.

AAC has prerequiste skills

The idea that Picture Exchange Communication System (PECS) is a prerequisite skill for Augmentative and Alternative Communication (AAC) is a myth. In fact, there are no prerequisite skills for high-tech and robust AAC! PECS was introduced in 1985 as a six-stage program to teach communication skills specifically to individuals with Autism Spectrum Disorder (ASD). There is a belief that PECS should be a prerequisite skill for an AAC device because it would give the individual a foundation on which to build more complex communication skills. However, research has shown that PECS is not a necessary prerequisite for AAC. There is no evidence to support the claim that an individual must complete the six-stage PECS program before they can benefit from using a robust AAC system. Any person whose communication needs are not met with speech or what they currently have could benefit from AAC and the SLP will make the determination of which system fits best.

Preventing Device Abandonment

If your learner has stopped using their AAC device, the first thing you should do is try to identify the reason why. AAC abandonment can be a frustrating phenomenon for everyone involved. However, by taking proactive steps to identify the reasons behind AAC abandonment and finding ways to address those issues, you can help your learner continue to make progress in their communication development.

There are a variety of reasons why AAC abandonment might occur. The first reason is that the individual might not have been given a choice. In many cases, the decision to use AAC is made by someone else (typically a Speech Language Pathologist or physician) without input from the individual who will be using the device. This can often lead to a feeling of powerlessness and resentment towards the device. Another reason why AAC abandonment might occur is simply because the individual finds the device too difficult to use. This could be due to inadequate training or support, lack of motivation, or cognitive or processing difficulties. Finally, some individuals or their families might feel that AAC devices are stigmatizing or embarrassing to use in public. There may be some cultural influences on this belief.

According to multiple studies, anywhere between 25 and 75% of people who use assistive technology devices stop using them within three years, and that the most frequently reported reasons for device abandonment were related to communication partner training and support issues. Some of the most noted reasons for device abandonment are listed below.

- Unrealistic expectations about the technology, followed by disappointment
- The device is not the best fit for the user
- A lack of training in how to use the devices
- Not offered ongoing maintenance or repair support
- The technology is too complex for the user's cognitive ability
- Social stigma
- Others believe it's not necessary

Fortunately, a few things can be done to reduce the risk of AAC abandonment. First and foremost, it is crucial to involve the individual in the entire decision-making process. This will help ensure that they feel empowered and motivated to use their device. Second, it is essential to provide adequate training so that the individual feels confident using their device and that their team is ready to support them. Finally, talking openly about any concerns about stigma or embarrassment can go a long way in helping the individual feel comfortable using their device in public. This may be a great opportunity for the individual or their family to join an AAC support group to discuss their concerns and learn from others on how to overcome their fears or hesitations.

Tips for preventing device abandonment

- Respect AAC user's choice in their AAC system. This is true even for very young learners. Often during the trialing phase of an AAC assessment, they may be given two or more systems to try. It's essential to recognize if they start showing preference towards one system over the other.

- Train the team! Initially, the SLP who completed the assessment is usually responsible for training the team on how to introduce AAC. Moving forward, other SLPs or AAC Specialists may take on the role of training the team members on how to use and expand AAC on an ongoing basis. Use the Collaboration Plan (page 142) to promote structured, individualized training.

- Make AAC fun! Incorporate AAC into your learner's favorite activities with no pressure to use it. Dr. Greg Hanley from the field of ABA has suggested that learning happens when individuals are "happy, calm, and engaged." If you pull out the AAC device and the AAC user runs or protests, unfortunately, the AAC system has already been established as "work." If this happens, go back to modeling (strategies will be taught later in the book), showing how AAC can make activities more fun without the expectation to communicate (ABA terminology: pairing).

- Create an upkeep plan. First, establish which team members will be responsible for maintaining the AAC device, including charging, troubleshooting, and backing up the device. Over time, these responsibilities should be taught to the AAC user to give them more independence (SLP terminology: operational competencies).

- Join or create a support group. Throughout the AAC journey, you may have many questions. Many people can relate! You can act as an AAC supporter by sharing education around myths to help normalize and accept the use of AAC. Whether you find more comfort in joining an already established AAC support group or starting your own with close friends and family, having a community of people to share experiences can help with the ongoing ups and downs of supporting an AAC user.

Getting an AAC Assessment

If you suspect that your loved one would benefit from Augmentative and Alternative Communication (AAC), it is important to advocate for them. There are various ways to obtain an AAC referral (see next page for infographic), and you may find that one path is more successful than another. However, no matter which route you take, persistence and collaboration are key.

One way to get an AAC assessment for your young child, birth through 3 years old, is through your state's early intervention programs that offer services for children with developmental delays or are at risk for developmental delays. For school-aged children, 3-21 years old, school districts are required to provide special education and related services to eligible children. You can request an evaluation through the school district's special education department. If it is determined that your child is eligible for special education services, the relevant service providers will develop an Individualized Education Program (IEP). The IEP will include a description of the student's current level of functioning as well as goals for the future. A speech-language evaluation should be included in the IEP if there is reason to believe your learner has a speech or language impairment. From there, an AAC referral can be made if needed.

The second way is to ask your Primary Care Physician (PCP). You can explain your concerns and ask if they would be willing to refer you to a Speech Language Pathologist (SLP) or other AAC specialist. It is helpful to come prepared with information about AAC, such as articles or brochures. You might also want to mention any concerns that may have led you to believe that your child would benefit from AAC services, such as difficulty communicating wants and needs, following verbal instructions, or communicating frustration.

Another option is to seek out private therapy providers in your area who specialize in AAC. This can be done by searching online or asking for recommendations from friends, family members, or other parents. Once you have compiled a list of potential providers, you can contact them directly and inquire about their AAC expertise and whether they are taking new clients.

For adults transitioning out of school to a vocational setting or independent living, there should be a new AAC assessment so that the device belonging to a school district can be replaced when the individual is over 21 years old and no longer served under an IEP. This AAC assessment should start during the Transition Planning component of their IEP. The AAC user should be involved in this process.

Lastly, service organizations or other non-profit organizations may be another avenue for obtaining funding for an AAC system.

There are many different paths that you can take in order to get an AAC referral and assessment for your learner. It is important to be persistent and provide plenty of information to your providers to understand the need for an AAC assessment and services. Collaboration between all parties involved—providers, families, and educators—is crucial in order to ensure success with AAC implementation.

Note: Each state, school district, and insurance provider may have different requirements and procedures, so make sure to check these out before starting your AAC assessment journey.

A Guide to Getting an AAC Assessment

Funding options for an AAC assessment

Initiation

Assessment

School

With this funding option, there is easier collaboration with educators, and the school district pays for the device/system and maintenance, repairs, and replacements.

Following a formal written request from the family, the school legally has to respond within 15 days, according to the Individuals with Disabilites Education Act (IDEA).

The school has 60 days for an SLP to complete the assessment with input from the IEP team.

Insurance

With this funding option, the family owns the AAC system and insurance can cover the cost of the device, maintenance, & repairs (with request from SLP).

Physician provides a referral for the assessment. The family seeks out an SLP to complete the assessment.

The SLP completes the assessment.
The assessment must include a 30 day trial of the recommended AAC systems and a follow-up report.

Private Pay

With this funding option, there is often faster access to services & equipment. The family is responsible for maintenance & repair.

The family seeks out an SLP to complete the assessment.

The SLP completes the assessment.

Vocational Rehabilitation

With this funding option, individuals own the AAC system. This route often starts during the Adult Transition Plan of an IEP.

The individual must qualify for vocational rehabilita tion services (federal). The vocational counselor provides a referral for the assessment and assists in seeking out an SLP to complete the assessment.

The SLP completes the assessment.

Assessment Report

Training & Services

Progress Report

The SLP/AAC assessment team presents the report in an IEP meeting and proposes recommended goals, services, and equipment.

❗ If the family or others in the IEP team do not agree with the assessment findings and recommendations, they can request an independent educational evaluation (IEE).

SLP provides ongoing training to family and school staff on communicative competencies and implementation of the AAC system in a way that promotes growth in IEP goals in natural environments.

An annual IEP meeting is held to report on progress and update goals and services. Typically, teachers and service providers send out progress reports quarterly.

The SLP shares the report with the family and the physician, including recommended goals, family-driven services, and durable medical equipment. The report must include a statement declaring no conflict of interest, ICD10 disability codes, as well as speech codes for billing purposes. With this funding route, all recommendations must be medically-based.

SLP provides training to family on communicative competencies and implementation of the AAC system.

❗ There is variation in service delivery, including ongoing therapy vs. an initial training and who provides the services.

SLP provides progress report to the family and insurance provider on a timeline determined by the insurance provider. The report should include proposed new goals and services.

The SLP shares the report with the family including recommended goals, services, and equipment. In order to provide the family with the most variety of funding options, the SLP should include all of the report requirements for insurance funding.

SLP provides training to family on communicative competencies and implementation of the AAC system.

❗ There is variation in service delivery including ongoing therapy vs. an initial training and who provides the services.

SLP provides progress report to the family. The report should include proposed new goals and services.

The SLP shares the report with the client and vocational rehabilitation counselor including recommended goals, services, and equipment. In order to provide the individual with the most variety of funding options, the SLP should include all of the report requirements for insurance funding with a focus on employment and independence.

SLP and the vocational rehabilitation counselor provide training to the individual on communicative competencies and implementation of the AAC system in a way that promotes employment and independence.

SLP provides progress report to the individual and employer. The report should include proposed new goals and services.

Introducing AAC

Let's Introduce AAC!

Now that you know more about AAC, you're ready to get started! This chapter will outline how best to introduce AAC into your learner's daily life. Then, with our recommended tips, you can feel confident that you are teaching AAC effectively and respectfully.

When introducing AAC, the first teaching phase is modeling, where you'll show your learner how to use the AAC system, but there's no expectation for them to use AAC to respond. You are just familiarizing them with the system and introducing common words in daily activities to start teaching language concepts. We'll provide two strategies for introducing communication through modeling: WOW (Word of the Week) and ACE (All Communication Expansion). Note that these are not official strategy names. We have simplified an evidence-based approach (Aided Language Input or Aided Language Stimulation) to be more approachable for new AAC supporters.

After introducing AAC and once the AAC user has started to show some interest in their AAC system (sometimes joining in), you'll move to the following strategies: WOW + Pause or ACE + Pause. Here, you will still be modeling but will add a little extra expectation by using a dramatic pause to indicate it's their turn to join in!

While there are specific AAC stages of language development, we have abbreviated them into three phases. This chapter covers phase 1 and phase 2, and the next chapter, "Further Expanding AAC," covers phase 3. If you would like more information about the stages of language development, reach out to your SLP.

Phase 1 Teaching: WOW or ACE
Phase 2 Teaching Plus: WOW + Pause or ACE + Pause
Phase 3 Independent communication

If you're starting with phase 1, meaning you are ready to introduce AAC to your learner for the first time, you'll want to pay particular attention to the tips outlined in this chapter. These tips help guide how to best teach AAC and how to communicate respectfully with our AAC users. Even those already supporting AAC users in their language development may learn new ideas on how to best communicate with AAC users!

Tip 1: Model more!
Tip 2: Use AAC to teach AAC
Tip 3: Choose individualized targets
Tip 4: Embody communication partner etiquette

Reminders: AAC is a team effort! Ensure that everyone who engages with the AAC learner has familiarized themselves with communication partner etiquette (page 65) and the AAC user's AAC system. Establish or review the Collaboration Plan (page 142) to ensure everyone is working cohesively to support the phase the AAC user is in. If there is particular information that stands out to you as being meaningful advice within our book, we recommend making a copy of that information to share with the team (e.g., Dos and Don'ts, Using AAC to Teach AAC, WOW and ACE, etc). While introducing AAC, it is essential to respect the AAC user's learning by presuming their competence and potential. We are excited for you to start introducing AAC!

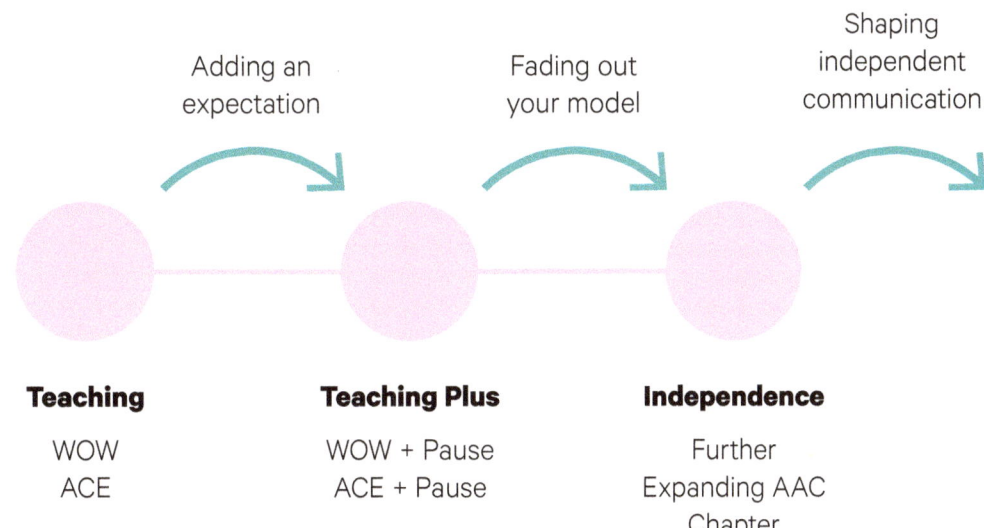

Teaching

WOW
ACE

Teaching Plus

WOW + Pause
ACE + Pause

Independence

Further
Expanding AAC
Chapter

Tip 1: Model more

Modeling is the most effective communication strategy for teaching AAC. Modeling is when a communication partner conveys a message using AAC rather than spoken words alone. There are different ways to model depending on the preferred communication mode. For example, it can look like exaggerating the target gestures/signs, pointing to symbols on a communication board, or activating a symbol or phrase on a speech-generating device while speaking the message out loud.

When modeling, you don't have to sign, point, or activate every word you say, especially in the beginning phases of introducing AAC. This will likely be too much for you as the communication partner and your user. Instead, "point & say" only the target words. This way, you highlight the word(s) that you are intentionally teaching without feeling overwhelmed by having to know and use hundreds of words straight from the beginning. For example, if you are targeting the word "see," you could vocally say, "I **SEE** Dad," but the only word that you would sign, point, or activate on a device would be the word "see." Here's another example of modeling along with speech: "It's time for snack! Let's **EAT**!" The only word you would model with AAC is "eat."

The more we model the use of AAC, the faster our AAC users will learn how to use their AAC system. In other words, modeling helps close the time gap between when our AAC learners are first exposed to AAC and when they are able to use it independently. Think of it like this: every minute spent modeling moves our AAC users closer to independence. If you expect the AAC user to communicate using their AAC system without taking the time to teach through modeling, you likely won't obtain the results you desire. We should not expect the AAC user to communicate if we have not shown them where their words are located or taught them the motor movements that create signs. The more we model, the more we teach—repetition is key! A bonus for modeling, beyond the benefits to the AAC user, is that the more we communicate using the AAC system, the better and more efficient we will also become at it! It is the fastest way to be an effective and efficient communication partner.

According to one study, the average typically developing child is exposed to oral language for approximately **4,380 waking hours** by the time they begin speaking at about 18 months. For an AAC user who gets speech services for 20-30 minutes each week, **it will take 84 years** to achieve the same level of exposure. This is why we need to model AAC for our AAC users: it helps to close that time gap and to expose them to their language.

We understand that many parents, caregivers, and teachers are extremely busy and overwhelmed. If you are just starting to model, model when you can. Ask other team members to join in the modeling efforts so that even if each person individually does a little bit of modeling every day, the cumulative effect can influence the overall impact.

In this illustration, we have shown an example of a way to incorporate modeling into your daily life. The dad has brought a printed core board to the grocery store and uses "point and say" to model "eat" for each item as he puts them in their cart. During this one errand, the dad created an engaging teaching activity by modeling the targeted word multiple times. Note: A core board is a paper with symbols of common ("core") words. We have created one in the Templates & Tools section, but you could also just print a screenshot of your learner's homepage of their AAC device.

As you become more familiar and comfortable with the AAC system, you can begin to model more. This may look like modeling during more activities or modeling new words or new word combinations. One way to incorporate more AAC is to model during daily routines such as leaving the house, recess, or morning/bedtime routines. For example, you can model "It's time to go!" every time you leave the house, "Ready, set, go!" before each time going down the slide, or singing a goodnight song with the AAC system to build repetition with these common phrases. No matter when or how you are modeling, it all positively impacts your AAC user.

Tip 2: Use AAC to teach AAC

To support our AAC users, we should use their AAC system to talk to them. Just like hearing children need exposure to spoken language to learn how to speak, AAC users need exposure to their AAC system to learn how to communicate with AAC. By modeling AAC systems, we are exposing our learners to their AAC language and can help them learn how to use it themselves. Remember that typically developing children are spoken to for an entire year before they start talking. AAC users need time to learn how to use their AAC device, and we should not expect an AAC user to be proficient in using their AAC system right away!

In the example below, the first row is how a neurotypical learner develops language where spoken language goes in (hearing), and spoken language comes out (speaking). The second row shows how AAC is sometimes taught: spoken language goes in (hearing), but AAC is the expected output (signing, pointing on a core board, activating a speech-generating device). This can be very confusing, frustrating, and not fair for the AAC user. You are asking them to translate spoken language into an AAC language they have never heard or seen before. Instead, we should be aiming for the third row. Here, AAC is the input, and AAC is the output! The best way to teach AAC is through AAC. This is modeling!

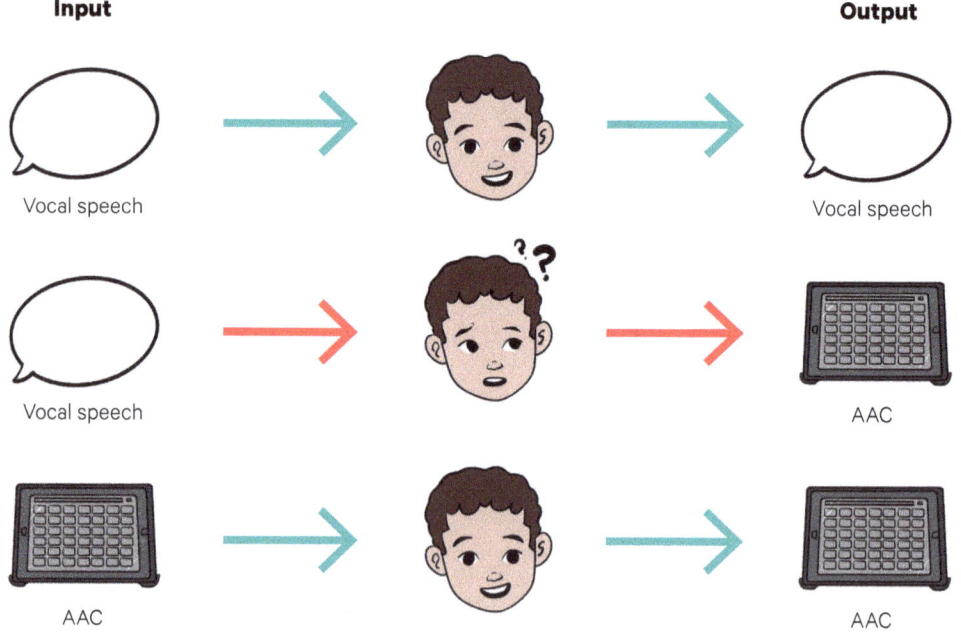

In the below illustration, the younger brother is using AAC to ask a question (AAC in), and his older brother is using AAC to respond (AAC out). This back-and-forth communication can be very helpful for those learning to use AAC. You can use AAC to communicate thoughts, opinions, and ideas—it is not solely about requesting. This will create more communication exchanges and give the AAC user more range in what they can communicate and express to people in their lives.

Note: As the AAC user becomes more and more independent and fluent with their AAC system, you using their system may start to feel too intrusive. Out of respect, you shouldn't touch someone's device or manipulate their hands to make a sign without their consent (or assent for individuals under 18 years old). If you notice they prefer for you not to use their device or assist them, this is a good sign! It likely means the AAC user has taken ownership of their AAC system (their voice), which can help with the longevity of the use of AAC. In this case, the communication partner should have their own AAC device to communicate with them. Ask your SLP for guidance on this process.

Tip 3: Choose individualized targets

Choosing which words to model first should be a team decision. Your SLP can help you determine if your learner would benefit from starting with words that have a lot of value to the AAC user (e.g., "blanket," "juice," "Mom") or words that have a lot of versatility (e.g., "like," "drink," "come"). Work together to decide on a list of "first words"! In the AAC world, these high value—but very specific—words are called "fringe words," and these common versatile words are called "core words."

The words we use most frequently in our lives are called "core words." They make up 80% of what we say. An easy way to think about core words is that many of them are the sight words that early readers learn first (e.g., "go," "see," "eat," and "you"). Core words are represented by verbs, prepositions, conjunctions, articles, adjectives, and pronouns. Nouns are less common. See page 138 for a 100 common core words list!

Core word vocabulary includes the words a person needs to communicate, express feelings, and be understood by others. This vocabulary has a lot of versatility across different situations and settings, so focusing on teaching core words often expands the AAC user's use of communication.

Fringe words are specific words that have a narrower meaning than core words. They describe particular things. Fringe words are more specific to a context or individual. They represent about 20% of our vocabulary. These words can only be used in certain situations, and they are not general words (e.g., "swing," "Dad," "yogurt," and "library").

Fringe words can be easier to teach because you can visualize them and explain them through pictures and icons. However, core words have more uses and practicality with communication partners. We can't just speak using fringe vocabulary, so core words must be emphasized.

The core word symbols should be kept in their current location in the AAC device or system and not moved or customized too much. However, fringe words are where AAC customization happens! By using words and phrases that are important to the AAC user and their family, customization can help in AAC acceptance. For example, if an AAC user's family has specific foods that are very important to them and their culture, that is where customization of fringe words can be made. On an AAC device, the fringe words can usually be found within the folders or pages behind the homepage. This is where you can edit the pre-loaded symbols for customized pictures of your AAC user's favorite things. Add personal pictures, family members, teachers, SLPs, ABA providers, favorite foods, toys, restaurants, shows, movies, special interests, and family traditions to align with your culture.

While it can be tempting to customize everything, try not to edit the home or main page. This is because a lot has already gone into creating your AAC user's AAC system. AAC language systems underwent a rigorous, research-based, and tested process to develop the AAC layout within your app or device. Everything from the placement of symbols, the colors used for the background or borders, and the layout are all very intentional. This has been designed for ease for the AAC user, and during the AAC assessment process, the SLP has determined which design is the best match for the AAC user. If you move around the icons, it would feel like someone took your phone, rearranged all your apps, and then expected you to be still as fluent in navigating through them.

This "motor planning" is like muscle memory. Let's say that you are a person who can type without looking. Imagine if someone rearranged all the letters on your keyboard. Your muscle memory would be useless. You would need to scan and select one letter at a time as you found them. This is what an AAC user may feel like if you rearrange their system. So try to keep the layout and core words exactly where they are within the AAC device or system; your AAC user and SLP will thank you for this.

Let's practice!

In the below conversation, try to find the core and fringe words. Then, turn to the next page to see how you did.

Mom: Do you want more bubbles?
Child: Yes! I want more!
Mom: Where do you want them?
Child: My head!
Mom: How fun! Bubbles on top!
Child: I like it!

Answer (core words are in bold)
Mom: **Do you want more** bubbles?
Child: **Yes! I want more!**
Mom: **Where do you want it?**
Child: **My** head!
Mom: **How** fun! Bubbles **on** top!
Child: **I like it**!

See how this feels like a natural conversation? That's because it's about 80% core and 20% fringe words. To help you become more familiar with core words, we have highlighted the core words within talk bubbles in bold font when you view the visual strategies in this book. We have also provided a list of the top 100 core words, as written by AAC Language Lab, within our Templates & Tools section (page 138).

Your turn!
Make a conversation script using 80% core/20% fringe words inspired by the below illustration.

Core words in the classroom

For teachers, incorporating AAC into a classroom can initially feel overwhelming. It feels like just one more thing added to an already very full plate.

We get it! "On top of managing students, classroom staff, challenging behaviors, IEP goals, potty training (for the early childhood folks), staff meetings, paperwork, parent communication, data collection, now you want me to learn a whole new communication strategy for one student and teach them how to use it all day?!"

We advise taking it one (core) word at a time. Focus on a single word throughout the day, like "Go." "Ready, set, go" when playing with cars or at recess, "Let's go!" when it's time to line up, "Go wash your hands," "Go check your schedule," or "Time to go home." This is the WOW strategy! (page 72) Throughout the school year, as you introduce a new word, add it to a word wall as you typically would do for sight words or vocabulary words. That way, all the staff in your classroom can quickly see which words the students should be familiar with to promote the maintenance of these words throughout the year.

Try to think of your classroom as a language immersion classroom. Some teachers have a dual immersion program incorporating English and another language into their teaching. We can take this same idea and apply the model to AAC. You can incorporate AAC into your structured teaching lessons, classroom norms, and routines. For early education, try picking songs with many core words and choosing stories with repetitive lines. You can adjust these songs and stories to focus on more core words. For example, in the nursery rhyme "5 Little Ducks," the actual lines are "5 little ducks went out one day. Over the hills and far away." To modify this to model more core words, you can sing, "5 little ducks went **out** one day. They **go up** and **down, up** and **down**," while modeling "**up** and **down**" on a core board or device and gesturing "up and down" with hand motions. Another idea that can work for students of any age is placing printed core boards around the classroom. This provides easier access to AAC language throughout the day and adds to the overall AAC immersion. If you point to "go" on a core board next to your classroom door every time you leave the classroom, there is a good chance that your students will begin to do the same.

AAC also has a positive impact on literacy skills. This is because using AAC requires many of the same skills necessary for reading and writing. For example, AAC individuals must be able to identify symbols representing words or concepts (pictorial symbol reading/writing) and understand how those symbols are organized (sequencing/syntax). In addition, they must be able to generate messages using those symbols (fluency/composition). The skills required for these tasks are similar to those needed for reading and writing, which means that individuals who use AAC devices may also be more likely to succeed in reading and writing tasks than those who do not use AAC devices.

If you start to see an AAC system as a teaching tool to teach communication for all of your students, it might feel a little more like an equitable use of your time and energy. AAC is a tool that will benefit more students than you think! Students with language delays, speech and language impairments, learning disabilities, or autism, as well as English language learners can benefit from visual support to learn language.

Tip 4: Embody communication partner etiquette

Communicating with AAC will look and feel different than vocal communication. There may be pauses while the AAC user is processing what you've said or as they come up with their response. While this may feel awkward initially, do not feel the need to fill the silent pauses, as this can be unintentionally impolite. It may take some time for the AAC user to compose their message, and patience is important during these moments. Do not finish their sentences for them or rush them along. Instead, wait patiently for them to finish so they can fully communicate their thoughts.

Always respect the personal space of others. Keep in mind that items such as wheelchairs, AAC devices, and other adaptations are a part of the personal space of people who use them. Therefore, checking in with people before touching or even assisting with their wheelchairs, AAC devices, and hands for d/Deaf and hard of hearing individuals is always polite.

When communicating, it's important to use open-ended questions. Open-ended questions cannot be answered simply by "yes" or "no," and they require the person to think creatively to answer. This type of question encourages your AAC user to use a broader range of vocabulary. Additionally, avoid interrupting the AAC user when they're trying to answer a question. This will help them feel heard and respected, which is essential for healthy communication.

Your tone of voice is an important cue for how the conversation is going. If you sound impatient or bored, the person using AAC will pick up on that and feel discouraged. Instead, try to sound natural and interested, as you would with any conversation partner. Avoid sounding forced or fake.

One thing that sometimes happens when modeling is that there starts to be an expectation that the AAC user is required to repeat exactly what was modeled. It's important to remember that the AAC user does not have to copy or repeat the words you have said or modeled. They can listen and see your words but do not need to repeat them with their AAC system or vocally. Instead, look for ways to engage and motivate them in fun activities. This will give them a chance to say something spontaneously, rather than demanding that they copy you. There should not be pressure to use AAC. AAC users are just like everyone else—they want to be heard and understood. By finding creative and fun ways to communicate with them, you are helping them do just that.

Final Dos and Don'ts

Dos

- Involve the AAC user in decision-making
- Form a collaborative team
- Join a support group or create your own
- Presume potential
- Always have the AAC system easily accessible and available
- Train the team on consistent AAC practices
- Have ongoing support from an SLP
- Model more
- Use AAC to teach AAC
- Focus on core words
- Find and create communication opportunities
- Honor all communication
- Provide wait time
- Allow AAC users to explore all the pages and icons
- Model comments over questions
- For early gestalt language processors: model in first person language ("I'm playing!")
- Make decisions based on data and team collaboration
- Prioritize connection and genuine communication
- Remain eternally curious about what your learner really has to say

Don'ts

- Expect the AAC user knows how to use the device to communicate
- Predict what the AAC user wants to say
- Introduce an app or system without SLP consult
- Change system or layout without SLP consult
- Only focus on requests
- Ask only "yes/no" questions
- Take the device away or leave it in a backpack or cubby
- Ask them to repeat themselves using the device if they have already communicated with a different mode
- Ask a lot of questions, especially "yes/no" questions
- Change or abandon systems and strategies without team input and data

Let's Start Teaching!

Now that you know all about AAC, it's time to implement it! We have illustrated two strategies for teaching AAC to your learner. If this is your first time using AAC with your learner, you may find that WOW is an easier starting point. But it is totally your choice! While "WOW" and "ACE" are not the official strategy names, they are based on AAC research and are both effective ways of introducing AAC.

Teaching

Start with Teaching. In both teaching strategies (WOW and ACE), it's all about modeling! Remember that modeling just means showing the AAC user how to communicate with their AAC system by using it yourself. For those that are using a core board or AAC device, just "point & say" to speak the target word as you are pointing to it (refer back to page 56-57). In this phase, you are exposing your learner to their AAC language. Think back to the fact that neurotypical children are exposed to a full year of vocal language before we expect them to talk. AAC users need time to be immersed in AAC too!

WOW stands for Word of the Week. In this teaching strategy, you select a target word and model it as much as possible for the whole week. Remember that it's a team effort, so get the entire team involved in modeling your WOW! Choosing your target word(s) should be a collaborative decision. We've created a planning form (page 130) to help boost your creativity in how to incorporate the WOW in your classroom, home, or therapy session.

The WOW strategy is great for repetition! As anyone who has ever learned a new language knows, repetition is key! The same is true when teaching AAC. Your AAC user will benefit from repeated exposure to the Word of the Week. Aim to target the word of the week 3-5 times in one situation.

One great way to incorporate the word of the week into your daily routine is to choose one activity that occurs throughout the day. For example, if you are working on teaching your child the word "drink," you could offer your child a drink multiple times throughout the day. Each time you offer your child a drink, say the word out loud and emphasize it while pointing to the word on your child's AAC device or picture card.

Incorporating the word of the week into daily activities is a great way to ensure that your child is getting plenty of exposure to the new word. Not only will they hear it multiple times, but they will also see it in different contexts and learn how to use it in different ways. This will help them to remember the new word and be able to use it more proficiently when they need it.

Our second teaching strategy is ACE: All Communication Expansion. We named it this to emphasize all the different communication that can happen during an activity. For example, in an art activity, you can request materials, comment about your artwork, ask questions to peers, and gain others' attention to share your masterpiece! Using this strategy, you are embedding AAC into something your learner already finds fun. On page 134, you'll find a planning form to help set up modeling opportunities during a chosen activity.

We communicate for all sorts of reasons. To make requests, get attention, share information, protest/reject, and share feelings. In the All Communication Expansion strategy, we can start modeling a variety of communication functions and vocabulary. This helps AAC users move beyond only making requests because you are modeling other reasons we communicate with a variety of core and fringe vocabulary.

In the field of Speech and Language Pathology, there are eight "communicative functions" (reasons we communicate): making requests, protesting, seeking information, stating preferences, commenting, interrupting, greeting/leaving, and self-regulation. Modeling all communicative functions will help AAC users expand their vocabulary so they can communicate beyond just making requests. It is important to show a variety of communicative functions so AAC users learn different ways to communicate with those around them!

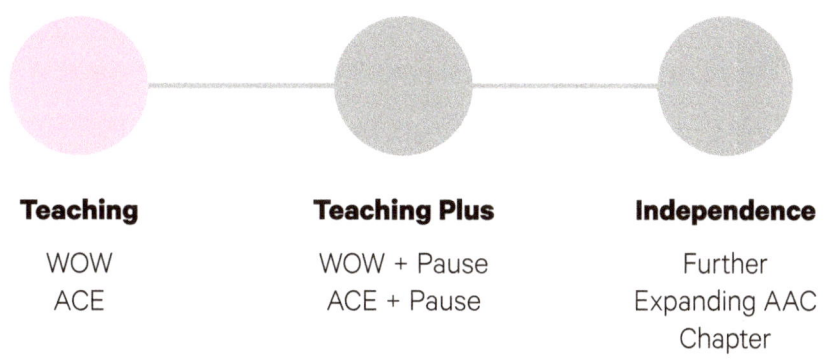

Teaching

WOW
ACE

Teaching Plus

WOW + Pause
ACE + Pause

Independence

Further
Expanding AAC
Chapter

Teaching Plus

You are ready to move to Teaching Plus when your learner has started to show interest in the AAC system by looking intently at your model and possibly joining in.

Teaching Plus is all about giving them an opportunity to communicate. You do this through "an expectant pause." Set up your WOW or ACE just as before, but now add a dramatic pause during the activity, providing them an opportunity to join in. This is a low-pressure way to encourage them to use AAC. If you pause and they do not respond, just keep modeling! You can always try again within that same activity. Now that they have an added expectation, you can start collecting data to measure progress. We have created a datasheet that can be found on page 150.

In true *AAC Visualized* style, we have included a few visual elements to enhance your understanding of the skills. On the next pages, you will see that the talk bubbles are color-coded to show different communication modes. Within the talk bubbles, we have bolded core words to help you further familiarize yourself with these versatile words. We have also labeled titles with the technical ABA and SLP jargon to highlight the collaborative approach further.

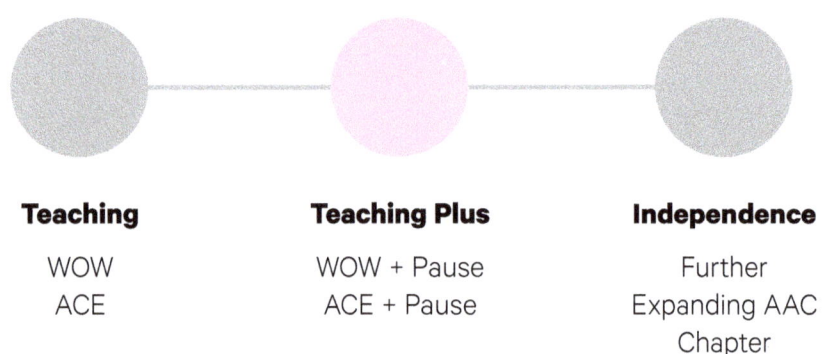

Teaching	**Teaching Plus**	**Independence**
WOW	WOW + Pause	Further
ACE	ACE + Pause	Expanding AAC
		Chapter

ABA terminology: Multiple exemplar training
SLP terminology: Aided language stimulation

WOW

Word of the Week:
Introducing communication

Goal

Teach the concept of common words.

How

Your turn! Choose one core word each week to model using AAC throughout the day in a variety of contexts, teaching the full concept of that word. Aim for 100 repetitions each day! This sounds like a lot, but it is a great opportunity for collaboration across all team members.

Context

Use this strategy for new AAC learners. During this phase, you are modeling, and there is no communication expectation from them. Each week, add a new WOW, creating a cumulative language repertoire.

Tip

Speak in full sentences, but only model the WOW using AAC. For those using core boards or AAC devices, remember this as "point & say!"

Legend

🗨 Vocal

🟪 ASL

🟦 AAC device & Core board

Bold text:
Core words

Standard text:
Fringe words

Choose one core word each week to model throughout different contexts, teaching the full concept of that word. Goal: 100x per day!

ABA terminology: Generalization
SLP terminology: Aided language stimulation
with expectant pause

WOW + Pause

Word of the Week:
Adding an expectation

Goal

Encourage their engagement in communication.

How

Their turn! Set up your WOW planning just as before,
but now add in an expectant pause. Model the
WOW, create a communication opportunity, then
pause! If they use AAC independently, celebrate by
enthusiastically repeating the word after they activated,
pointed to, or signed it. This gives one more repetition
of that word through validation instead of saying
"good job" or "you did it!" which can be more effective
at teaching this new skill. If they don't communicate
following your model, that's ok! Just keeping modeling.

Context

Use this strategy with AAC users who are starting
to show interest in their AAC system and may be
attempting AAC on their own. This timeline is different
for everyone!

Tip

Be patient & flexible. If they press the wrong button
or the sign is not perfect, that's ok! If this happens,
model communication that fits the context one more
time.

Legend

🗨 Vocal

🟪 ASL

🟦 AAC device
& Core board

Bold text:
Core words

Standard text:
Fringe words

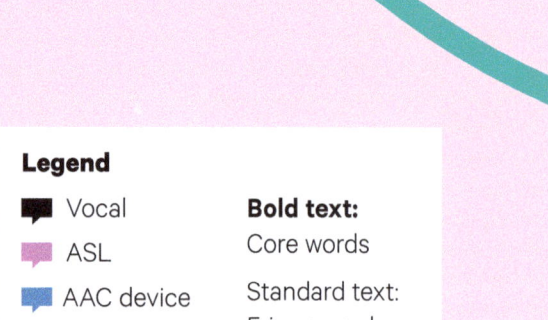

Throughout the day in different contexts, continue modeling the WOW, but now add a pause indicating it's their turn to try!

ACE

All Communication Expansion:
Introducing communication

Goal

Teach the versatility of communication.

How

Your turn! Choose one activity each day to focus on modeling the full range of communication (i.e. requests, comments, rejections, emotions, etc) within that activity. During this activity, model using AAC for all of your communication. We want to teach that language can make their favorite activities even more fun!

Context

Use this strategy for learners who are already attending to your use of AAC and possibly already responding or requesting with AAC. During this phase, you are modeling, and there is no communication expectation from them.

Tip

Aim for 80/20 (80% core, 20% fringe, see page 60). When choosing what language to model, prioritize using core words (see page 130 for planning form). This is a great way to build your own fluency as you model more words and introduce fringe words.

Let's **get** started!

get

Legend

🗨 Vocal

🗨 ASL

🗨 AAC device
& Core board

Bold text:
Core words

Standard text:
Fringe words

During one activity, model AAC prioritizing the use of core words and phrases, teaching the versatility of communication.

ABA terminology: Teaching across the verbal operants with data collection
SLP terminology: Teaching different communicative functions with added expectation

ACE + Pause

All Communication Expansion: Adding an expectation

Goal

Encourage their engagement in expanded communication.

How

Their turn! Set up your ACE planning just as before, but now add in an expectant pause. Throughout the activity, model using AAC, create a communication opportunity, then pause! If they use AAC independently, celebrate! If not, continue teaching through modeling.

Context

Use this strategy once the learner has shown interest and possibly started copying some of your modeled language in Teaching: ACE.

Tip

Follow their lead! Use this strategy during activities that are of high interest to them. It's helpful if you choose activities that have multiple parts or steps so that it's easier to create communication opportunities.

1

Look! New paints!

Look!

Model communication

During a preferred activity, model different phrases, making the activity even more fun!

Legend

🔲 Vocal

🟪 ASL

🟦 AAC device & Core board

Bold text:
Core words

Standard text:
Fringe words

Create a communication opportunity

While they're engaged, create motivation by setting up the activity in a way that encourages communication. Signal that it's their turn to communicate.

Their turn!

As soon as they communicate, make sure to repeat the communication back to them in acknowledgment, and celebrate!

Further Expanding AAC

Introduction

Once your AAC user is consistently filling in the pauses and starting to spontaneously initiate communication, you are ready to support expanding AAC! In this chapter, we'll outline the framework of how to expand AAC with your AAC user, ultimately leading towards their independence in communication!

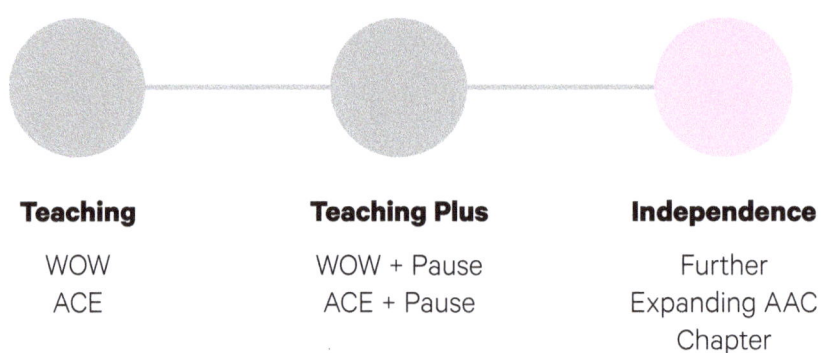

Teaching	**Teaching Plus**	**Independence**
WOW	WOW + Pause	Further
ACE	ACE + Pause	Expanding AAC
		Chapter

Expanding communication

There are three strategies to expand upon communication. First, we can expand one word requests that your AAC user is already making by teaching additional descriptive words like big, small, and color words ("big + truck") or adding an action ("help + open"). The second way to expand communication is focusing on all of the different reasons we communicate beyond requesting. Often, we observe an excessive dependency on the use of AAC for requesting. This is especially true in the early stages of implementation. However, there is so much more to communication than just wants and needs. Shift your focus to building other communication areas like social commenting, expressing emotions, and self-advocacy. And finally, you can expand your responses to longer phrases and sentences as a model of more advanced communication.

1. Using descriptive commenting

Descriptive commenting is a great way to expand your AAC user's communication repertoire and help them use AAC for a variety of purposes. Descriptive commenting is exactly what it sounds like—adding adjectives, colors, size, or quality words to comments. For example, instead of just saying "juice," you might say "red juice" or "sweet juice." This may seem like a minor change, but it can make a big difference in your learner's ability to communicate effectively and expand on their communication skills. Try choosing descriptive words as a WOW! Model big/small in a variety of contexts throughout the day to teach these concepts. For each of the visual strategies in this chapter, consider your AAC user's communication level. Initially, they might be requesting social connection by communicating "come look." You could expand on this with descriptive commenting by modeling, "Come look! It's silly!"

Tips for using descriptive commenting

Here are a few tips for incorporating descriptive commenting into your learner's AAC system:

- Keep it simple at first. Add one or two adjectives to your AAC users request and expand from there as the AAC user becomes more comfortable with the concept.
- Be consistent. Once you start using descriptive commenting, try to use it as often as possible so that they get used to hearing it.
- Get creative. In addition to obvious adjectives like "big" or "small," get creative with your descriptions. For example, you might describe something as "sparkly" or "squishy."
- Describe emotions and intentions. In addition to describing physical characteristics, try describing emotions and intention (e.g., "I'm feeling happy" or "I want some juice").
- Use props whenever possible. Props can be a great way to help illustrate descriptive words (e.g., holding up a green shirt while saying "green shirt").
- Give praise when warranted. Whenever your AAC user uses descriptive commenting effectively, be sure to give them lots of praise! This will encourage them to keep using this important skill.

2. Moving beyond requests

The second way to expand AAC use is by moving beyond requests. There are many reasons we communicate, like commenting, asking and answering questions, social closeness (like greetings, sharing personal information, joking), and rejecting or protesting. Even very young AAC users have more to say than their wants and needs!

On page 87, you can see which skills we recommend to start with based on your overall communication goals. So for example, if your collaborative team has identified that building social skills would be beneficial for your AAC user, you could prioritize teaching social commenting or asking clarifying questions with peers. If you'd like to have a better understanding of what communication skills your AAC user is already independent in versus what areas could be identified for communication growth, we've listed the skills as a checklist on page 146 that you can complete with your team.

3. Expanding your responses

Another way to help your AAC user expand their communication is to expand your responses. An easy way to remember this is to "one up" their communication. If they communicate "like," while pointing at a puzzle, you can add one word to respond back with something like, "like puzzle." Or if they communicated "I like this one!" you can add one word to respond back with, "I remember you like this one!" You can use this strategy as a low pressure way to expand communication with any of the communication skills.

Using these three strategies will help your AAC user add more vocabulary, move beyond requests, and have more exposure to language throughout their day.

Expanding functional communication

To support AAC users in becoming totally independent in their communication, we can "shape" or "expand" their communication skills by gradually building upon skills they are already showing. We recognize that expanding AAC is not going to be a perfect, seamless process. Challenging behaviors may occur. The good news is that there is substantial research across ABA, speech, and education fields that shows that building functional communication is the most effective way at reducing challenging behaviors. When your learner is engaging in challenging behaviors, this is their way of communicating something to you in that moment. In ABA, this is what is called the functions of behavior. Think back to the last time your learner had a challenging behavior. What were they trying to communicate to you in that moment?

Escape

- "I'm not ready yet"
- "I don't want to"
- "It's too hard"
- "I don't know how"

Attention

- "My friends think this is funny"
- "I want to show you something"
- "I think it's funny when my parent/teacher yells"
- "Talk to me too!"

Access

- "I don't want to share"
- "I want that"
- "I'm not done playing yet"
- "I want it now"

Sensory

- "This feels good"
- "I feel like I need to do this"
- "This looks cool"
- "This relaxes me"

By teaching phrases like these, you are giving your learner the tools to communicate their needs in a more acceptable way. This is called Functional Communication Training (FCT). While there are many ways to teach someone these replacement phrases (i.e. textual prompts, role play, visual supports, video modeling), in AAC, we typically want to use modeling. Look back to page 56 to read more about the benefits of modeling within AAC.

A tip that provides easier access to these phrases is to work with your SLP to set up a pre-programmed phrase within the AAC device or have an abbreviated sign. It's essential that in moments of need, the AAC user can quickly and easily communicate with the replacement word/phrase to prevent challenging behaviors (ABA jargon: matching law).

Putting it all together

In the visualized communication skills within this chapter, you will see many follow an outline of a communication opportunity leading to communication, which leads to a communication outcome. For those familiar with ABA, you may recognize this as "ABC," standing for Antecedent, Behavior, Consequence. Recognizing the communication opportunity for the skill you are trying to build is essential, as this is where teaching should occur for new skills. As a communication opportunity arises, model the replacement phrase (communication skill) to teach that it can lead to the communication outcome, the reward! For each skill we have visualized, we provided sample teaching targets that you could model to promote this skill-building. Over time, you can fade out your modeling, allowing the learner to recognize the communication opportunity on their own and independently communicate.

Even with all this teaching and effort, there may be missed communication opportunities and challenging behaviors may still occur. Start by familiarizing yourself with the Supporting Communication visual strategy within this chapter. This is your plan when your first plan doesn't work! Within the communication skills visualized in this chapter, you will see an indication to return back to this Supporting Communication visual strategy in the case that the AAC user needs more support. You'll need to adjust the specifics to align to the communication skill; however the steps will be the same.

Use the Skills Checklist on page 146 to identify with your team which skills to target first. The graphic on the right can help you choose which skills align with your long-term goals. You can choose whichever ones you want in whichever order. This is totally based on the individual needs of your AAC learner.

In order to guide you through choosing which communication skill is best suited for your individual AAC learner, we organized all the featured communication skills by their connection to long term goals. Find your AAC user's goal on the left side of the chart, and follow the lines to identify which strategy may be effective at reaching this goal. It is important to know that multiple strategies may be beneficial, and we encourage you to try them all to see which combination leads to positive results for you and your AAC learner. Remember that repetition and consistency are key, so when you choose a communication skill, practice it multiple times a day and get the whole team to practice too! We've also created Sample Goals (page 148) that align with each skill. Check off the skills on the checklist as your AAC user learns them!

Overall goal

Communication skill

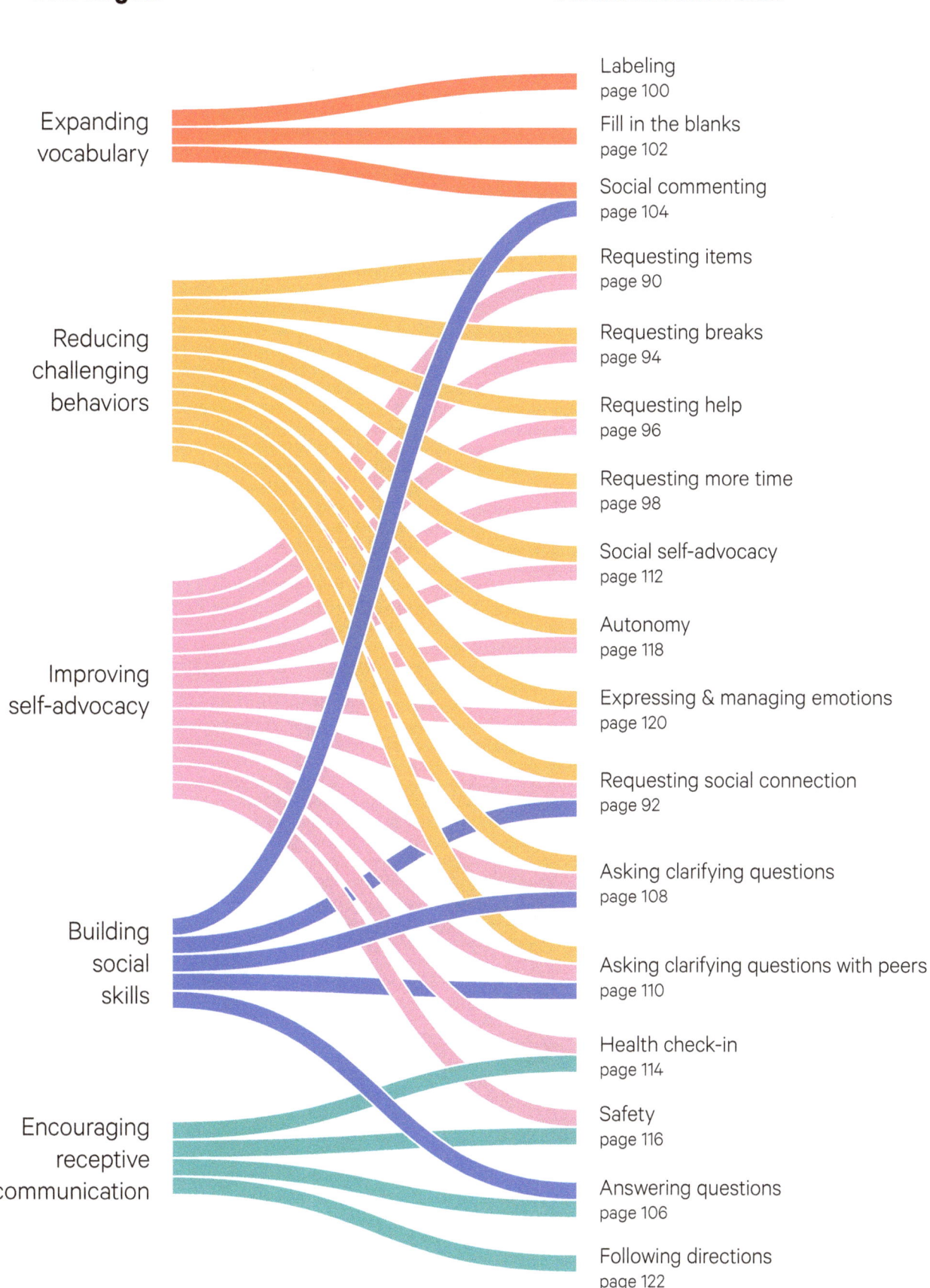

Expanding
vocabulary

Reducing
challenging
behaviors

Improving
self-advocacy

Building
social
skills

Encouraging
receptive
communication

Labeling
page 100

Fill in the blanks
page 102

Social commenting
page 104

Requesting items
page 90

Requesting breaks
page 94

Requesting help
page 96

Requesting more time
page 98

Social self-advocacy
page 112

Autonomy
page 118

Expressing & managing emotions
page 120

Requesting social connection
page 92

Asking clarifying questions
page 108

Asking clarifying questions with peers
page 110

Health check-in
page 114

Safety
page 116

Answering questions
page 106

Following directions
page 122

Supporting Communication

ABA terminology: Extinction + redirection to functional communication with differential reinforcement
SLP terminology: Aided language + redirection

Goal

Turn a missed opportunity into a teaching moment.

How

When a learner misses an opportunity to use AAC to communicate, we want to first validate their attempted communication, then model for them how to use AAC in that moment.

Context

In this chapter you will learn how to promote AAC across all different contexts. While your AAC user is learning these skills, they will likely need some support. Return back to this page often and follow the steps in the context of that particular skill.

Tip

Although we want to recognize & reward when the AAC user learns from this missed opportunity, the celebration should not be as big or rewarding as when they do this skill independently (ABA terminology: differential reinforcement).

Communication opportunity

Recognize a moment where the learner may want to communicate with you or others.

Legend

🗨 Vocal

🗨 ASL

🗨 AAC device & Core board

Bold text: Core words

Standard text: Fringe words

Model

Show them how they can better communicate in that moment.

Communication

AAC user communicates independently.

Communication outcome

Respond to their communication enthusiastically! We want to celebrate all independent communication, especially for new AAC users.

Missed opportunity

The learner may attempt other ways to communicate such as engaging in challenging behaviors or pulling others towards something.

Validate

Recognize their communication attempt and feelings in this moment.

Retry

Give them one more opportunity to try again using AAC. You may need to provide a little more assistance here.

Reward!

Recognize & respond to their communication, but not as enthusiastically as if they had done it independently.

Requesting Items

Goal

Build vocabulary of common/preferred items.

How

For early learners, create a communication opportunity by placing a preferred item just out of reach, but in sight. Try only putting out a few toys to build their motivation to ask for more! Pause to give the AAC user an opportunity to request independently. If they request, give them what they asked for! If they don't, turn this into a learning opportunity through modeling (page 88).

Context

For many learners, teaching how to request items can be a replacement skill for challenging behaviors.
If your learner pulls on you or often has tantrums when they want something, teaching how to use AAC to request their needs throughout the day can be greatly beneficial!

Tip

Over time, start putting preferred items away throughout the day so that the AAC user can learn to request items that are out of sight.

Communication opportunity

Place a preferred item just out of reach, but in sight.

Teaching targets

- can
- have
- will
- want
- need
- like

Communication

AAC user requests item independently.

Communication outcome

Give them what they asked for!

Missed opportunity

Other attempts of getting the item such as climbing on someone or furniture, grabbing it from someone, or other challenging behaviors may occur.

Go to page 88

Legend

🖤 Vocal

🟪 ASL

🟦 PECS

Bold text:
Core words

Standard text:
Fringe words

ABA terminology: Manding attention
SLP terminology: Pragmatics or social language

Requesting Social Connection

Goal

Build vocabulary of social activities.

How

To teach, contrive a communication opportunity where you are nearby, but not currently giving them attention (you are engaged in something else). Pause to give the AAC user an opportunity to request your attention. If they request, stop what you are doing and shift your focus to them! If they don't, turn this into a learning opportunity through modeling (page 88).

Context

Diverted attention, or being present but your attention is elsewhere, is a common trigger for many learners. Teach your learner to use AAC to request hugs, tickles, listening to a story, or any other types of social attention that your learner loves.

Tip

Expand this skill with peers! Use modeling to teach social phrases like "Come play with me" or "Want to play ____?" when they are with classmates/friends/family members.

Communication opportunity

Diverted attention: you or peers are nearby, but are engaged in something else.

Teaching targets

- I/me/you
- come
- look
- want
- need
- like
- play

Communication

AAC user requests attention independently.

Communication outcome

Shift your focus to them! Give the type of social engagement they requested.

Missed opportunity

Other attempts of gaining attention such as pulling on someone or other challenging behaviors may occur.

Go to page 88

Legend

🗨 Vocal

🟪 ASL

🟦 AAC device & Core board

Bold text:
Core words

Standard text:
Fringe words

ABA terminology: Manding escape
SLP terminology: Requesting self-regulation

Requesting Breaks

Goal

Self-advocate during challenging activities.

How

Identify activities that are typically challenging or tiresome for your learner. At the first signs of distress, give the AAC user an opportunity to request a break independently. If they request a break, remove the current task or allow them to leave the work area. If they don't, turn this into a learning opportunity through modeling (page 88).

Context

Prior to introducing activities that are particularly difficult for your learner, remind them of how they can request a break if needed using their preferred AAC method. This will look different across ages! Consider using visual break cards, text/email, signs, and more.

Tip

1. Combine this strategy with teaching expressing & managing emotions (page 120)! Model for the AAC user how to identify emotions and use coping skills during their break.
2. Look up the average attention span for your learner's age to determine how often they may need a break.

Communication opportunity

Know your learner! Opportunities to take a break could include when they've reached their typical duration of sustained attention or when a task is challenging.

Teaching targets

- stop
- finished/all done
- need
- feel
- now
- away

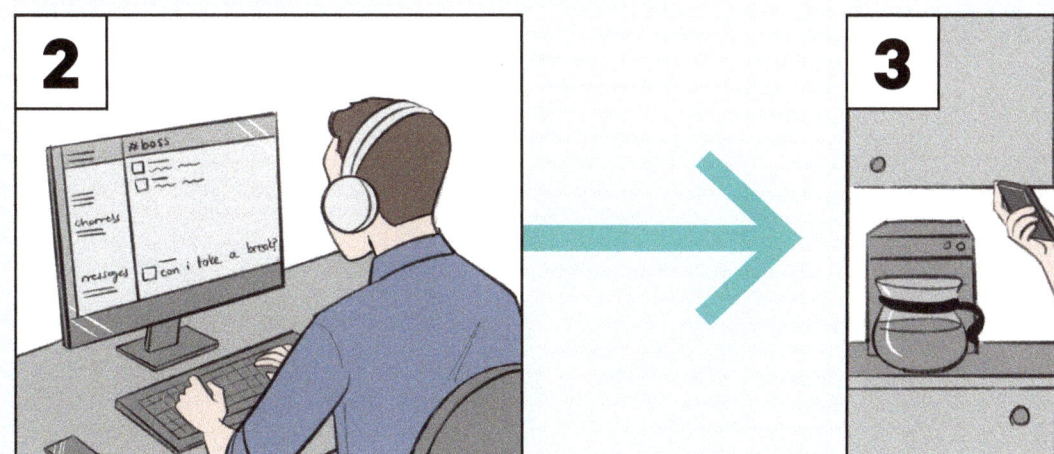

Communication

AAC user requests for a break
independently.

Communication outcome

Briefly remove the task or allow them to
leave the work area.

Missed opportunity

Stopping engagement in the activity
(e.g. putting head down, pushing task
away), increased distress, or challenging
behavior may occur.

Go to page 88

Legend

🗨 Vocal   **Bold text:**
Core words

🟪 ASL

🟦 AAC device   Standard text:
& Core board   Fringe words

Requesting Help

Goal

Self-advocate for assistance.

How

Identify activities that your learner often needs assistance to complete. During these activities, give the AAC user an opportunity to request help independently. If they request, immediately provide assistance. If they do not request, turn this into a learning opportunity through modeling (page 88).

Context

Requesting help is an essential skill to learn for safety and independence within the community. From the beginning when introducing this skill, teach the versatility of "help" across many contexts, settings, and people.

Tip

To start, teach the one word request, "help." Next, some learners may learn "help" + point (to what they need help with). Over time, build in more specific (fringe) vocabulary like "help open," "help cut," and "help fix."

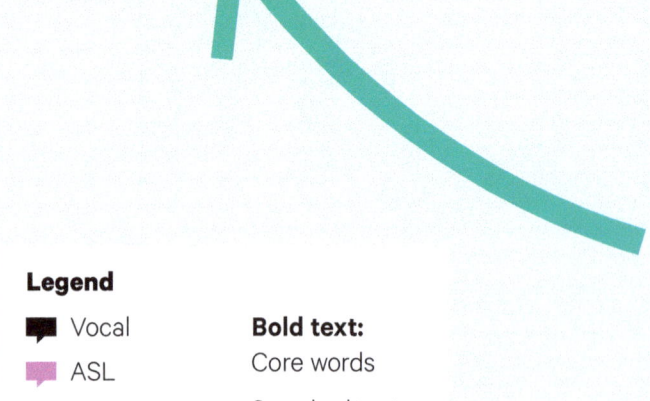

Legend

🗨 Vocal

🟪 ASL

🟦 AAC device & Core board

Bold text:
Core words

Standard text:
Fringe words

As the skill of requesting help is essential for safety and independence, get everyone involved! Use WOW strategy (page 72) to teach "help," then expand (fringe) vocabulary to make specific requests.

Requesting More Time

Communication opportunity

An instruction to stop a preferred activity or transition to another activity, when they are not quite ready.

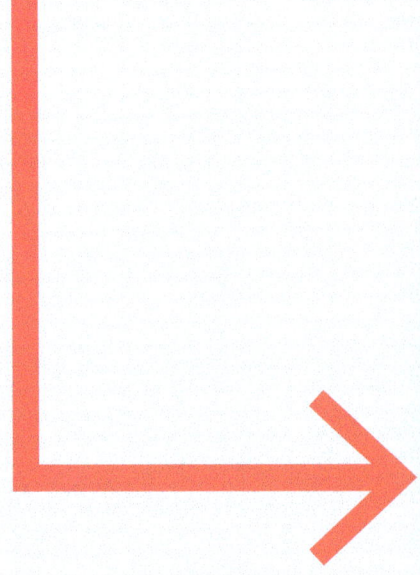

Goal

Create smoother transitions.

How

Identify transitions that are typically challenging for your learner. Following the transition instruction, give the AAC user an opportunity to request more time independently (e.g., "more time please," "can I have 2 more minutes?," "can I finish this game?"). If they request, provide a few more minutes (2-5 min recommended) for them to complete the activity. If they do not request more time or transition, turn this into a learning opportunity through modeling (page 88).

Context

Transitions are tricky! They typically involve two instructions: stopping a preferred activity and starting a non-preferred activity. Prior to these tricky transitions, remind your AAC user that they can ask for more time if needed.

Tip

When teaching this skill, we want to honor their request every time. A clever trick to help you honor this request is to end the activity a few minutes earlier than you initially intended. That way, when they ask for more time, the transition is happening when you had originally planned!

Teaching targets

- more
- again
- now
- not all done / not finished
- need
- want
- can
- have

Communication

AAC user requests more time independently.

Communication outcome

Allow a few more minutes to engage in the activity, then follow through with the transition instruction.

Missed opportunity

Challenging behavior may occur.

Go to page 88

Legend

▪ Vocal		**Bold text:** Core words
▪ ASL		Standard text: Fringe words
▪ AAC device & Core board		

Labeling

Goal

Expand vocabulary.

How

Identify activities that your learner already enjoys, considering if your learner is more attentive to 2D pictures/books or 3D items. Think of vocabulary that could be labeled with the 5 senses (i.e., sight, smell, feel). While engaged in the activity, draw their attention to what you want them to label (e.g., by pointing to something, gesturing to your ear, or holding something up). Give the AAC user an opportunity to label independently. If they do, provide praise & continue the social engagement. If they do not, turn this into a learning opportunity through modeling (page 88).

Context

Make it fun! Complete a puzzle then take turns labeling what is in the image, play "I Spy" while on a walk outside, use illustrative books on topics that your learner loves, or incorporate labeling the weather into a circle time song.

Note: For early gestalt language processors, they may more easily label using a whole phrase.

Tip

To enhance learning, after the AAC user has labeled, use their AAC method to confirm the vocabulary ("Yes! That is a flower!").

Look at **this** new card **I got!**

Communication opportunity

Draw their attention to something you want them to label. Later, spontaneous labeling may occur within the communication opportunity of just seeing interesting things that they want to talk about!

Teaching targets

- it
- is
- this
- that
- look

- colors
- big / little
- fast / slow
- same / different
- new / old

Communication

The AAC user labels the item. Over time, one word labels will expand into 2-3 words, then into full descriptive sentences!

Communication outcome

Continue the social engagement! To enhance early learning of this skill, confirm the vocabulary using their AAC method.

Missed opportunity

No back & forth communication may occur, resulting in a pause in the social engagement.

Go to page 88

Legend

■ Vocal		**Bold text:** Core words
■ ASL		Standard text: Fringe words
■ AAC device & Core board		

Fill in the Blanks

Goal

Introducing shared communication.

How

Choose recognizable lyrics or phrases that can be incorporated in play (e.g. "1, 2,...," "Head, shoulders, knees, and..."). Using a very animated and playful tone, say the first part of the phrase, then do a dramatic pause to indicate that it is their turn to finish the phrase. If they continue the phrase, enthusiastically continue social engagement. If they do not, turn this into a learning opportunity through modeling (page 88).

Context

Practice this skill during songs where you can easily pause and restart the music. You can also practice this with social play activities like spinning around together or with cause-and-effect toys and activities (e.g., pushing a car down a ramp or pushing them on the swing/slide: "Ready, set,...gooo!!"). To enhance literacy skills, pick a book that has repetitive phrases and leave the last line for them!

Note: This skill is not a good choice for early gestalt language processors.

Tip

When teaching sign language, exaggerate your signs by bouncing them in a playful manner by rhythmically moving your hands up and down and repeating the signs 2-3 times.

Communication opportunity

The start of a recognizable phrase + pause.

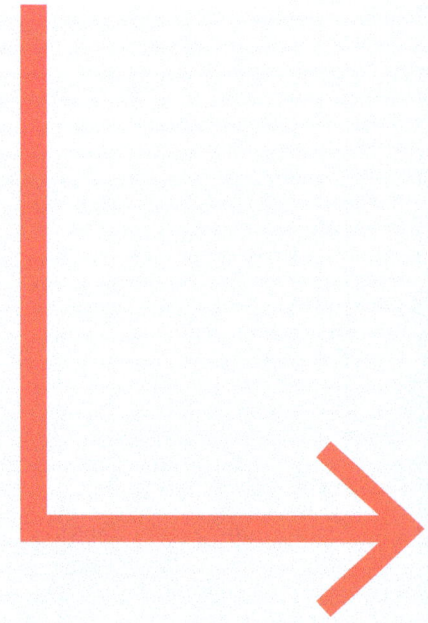

Teaching targets

- go
- my turn / your turn
- up / down
- on / off
- fast / slow

Communication

AAC user independently finishes the phrase.

Communication outcome

Social engagement continues! Make the fill-in phrase part of the activity for even more fun.

Missed opportunity

No response or challenging behaviors may occur.

Go to page 88

Legend

Vocal	**Bold text:**	
ASL	Core words	
AAC device & Core board	Standard text: Fringe words	

Social Commenting

Goal

Develop early conversational skills.

How

Same, same, different! During a partner or small group activity, have the communication partner make a statement about the activity. Pause the activity to give the AAC user an opportunity make a similar comment back. If they create their own social comment, provide praise & continue the social engagement. If they do not, turn this into a learning opportunity through modeling (page 88).

Context

This strategy works best during preferred activities so that the AAC user has more motivation to communicate. If there are multiple people present, try going around in a circle to create more modeling opportunities prior to the AAC user's turn (e.g., "I drew a bird," "I drew a fish," "I drew my Mom!").

Tip

If your learner tends to copy what they have heard (scripting or echolalia), this strategy could be a great way for them to use this as a strength! In each phrase, most words are repeated, but when novel language is added, a conversation is happening! Refer to gestalt language on page 34.

Communication opportunity

Someone makes a comment in a social setting.

Teaching targets

- I/mine/you
- like
- make
- see
- feel
- same / different
- pretty

Communication

AAC user makes a similar, related comment in response.

Communication outcome

Social engagement continues!

Missed opportunity

No response or challenging behaviors may occur.

Go to page 88

Legend

■ Vocal		**Bold text:** Core words
■ ASL		
■ AAC device & Core board		Standard text: Fringe words

Answering Questions

Communication opportunity

The AAC user is asked a question.

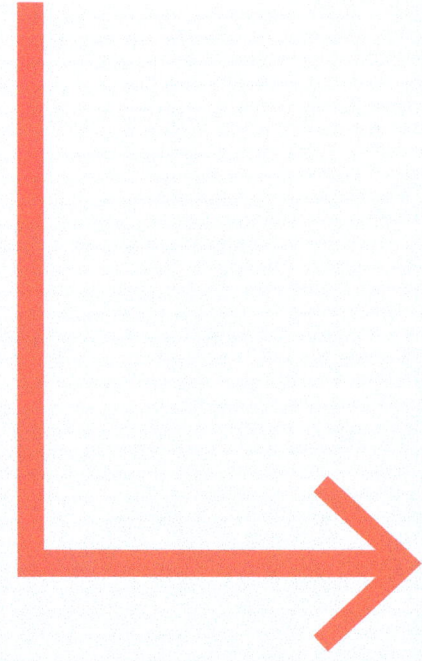

Goal

Build confidence in back & forth communication.

How

Following a question being asked, pause to give the AAC user an opportunity to answer the question. If they answer the question, validate their response and continue the social engagement! If they do not, turn this into a learning opportunity through modeling (page 88).

Context

Answering questions can be tricky, as there are many different questions that your learner may be asked throughout the day! When teaching this skill, choose a few common questions to practice before expanding. For early AAC learners, try asking the question with their AAC system! What if they answer "incorrectly"? See FAQs on page 125.

Tip

For common personal information questions, collaborate with SLP to create a phrase within the AAC device such as "I'm 5 years old" or "My address is 1210 Kokomo St."

Teaching targets

- yes / no
- like / don't like
- eat / drink
- want
- help
- let's (go / eat / play / do)

Communication

AAC user independently answers the question. Note: if they answer incorrectly, that's okay! We're initially teaching & rewarding any attempts of back and forth communication. If this happens, validate their response and model the "correct" answer on their AAC system.

Communication outcome

While asking & answering questions is a very versatile skill, the overall goal is to teach that communicating can be fun & effective for getting needs met.

Missed opportunity

No response or challenging behaviors may occur.

Go to page 88

Legend

■ Vocal
■ ASL
■ AAC device & Core board

Bold text:
Core words

Standard text:
Fringe words

Asking Clarifying Questions

Goal

Build self-advocacy in gaining information.

How

When an unexpected or unclear situation arises, at first signs of confusion, pause to give the AAC user an opportunity to ask a question. If they ask a question to gain information, immediately tell them the information (preferably using their AAC method)! If they don't, turn this into a learning opportunity through modeling (page 88).

Context

Common opportunities for someone to ask questions include a change in schedule, a family member not being home at the usual time, an assignment being given in the classroom with unclear instructions, etc. Instead of jumping in to give the information, teach them how to ask!

Tip

When teaching this skill, use repetition of the "Wh-" questions. Try using "where" or "why" as your WOW!

Communication opportunity

A vague situation or instruction.

Teaching targets

- what
- when
- where
- who
- why
- how

Communication

AAC user asks a "Wh-" question to gain information.

Communication outcome

Respond with the requested information, preferably using their AAC method.

Missed opportunity

No response or challenging behaviors may occur.

Go to page 88

Legend

- ▬ Vocal
- ▬ ASL
- ▬ AAC device & Core board

Bold text: Core words

Standard text: Fringe words

ABA terminology: Manding for information
SLP terminology: Peer-based instruction intervention

Asking Clarifying Questions with Peers

Goal

Build self-advocacy in gaining information from peers.

How

This strategy set-up is the same as the previous, however now we are creating opportunities for the AAC user to communicate with peers throughout the day. Do this by establishing a communication partner: a peer who can recognize and support the AAC user's communication.

Context

If you have an AAC user in your classroom, this strategy is for you! Other opportunities to promote social communication with peers include siblings at home, with other family members, in group services, and during community outings.

Tip

1. Use our communication partner etiquette tips (page 65) to help promote effective peer communication!
2. Customize AAC device by adding in common slang and trending topics.

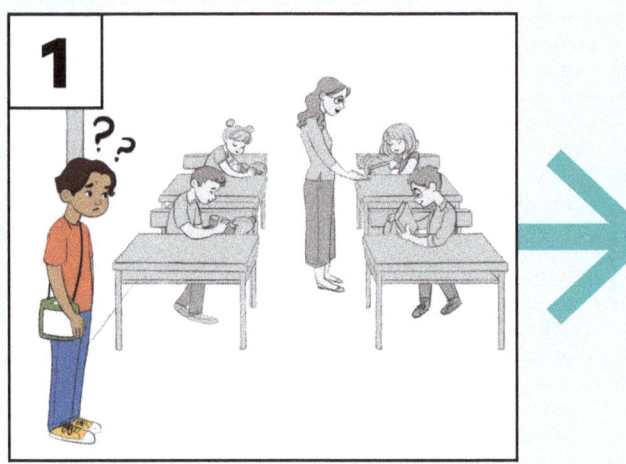

Communication opportunity

A vague situation or instruction.

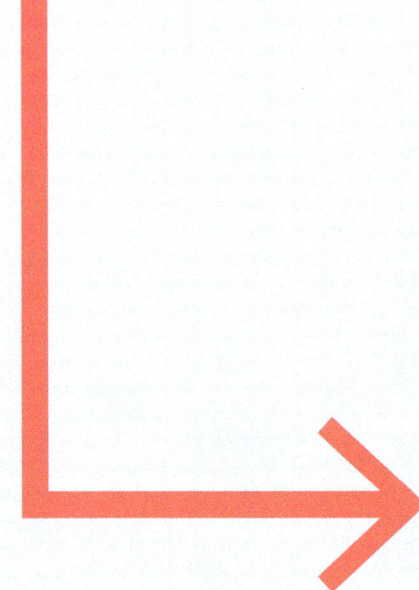

Teaching targets

- what
- when
- where
- who
- why
- how

Communication

AAC user asks a peer a "Wh-" question to gain information.

Communication outcome

With the provided information, the AAC user is included in the social situation.

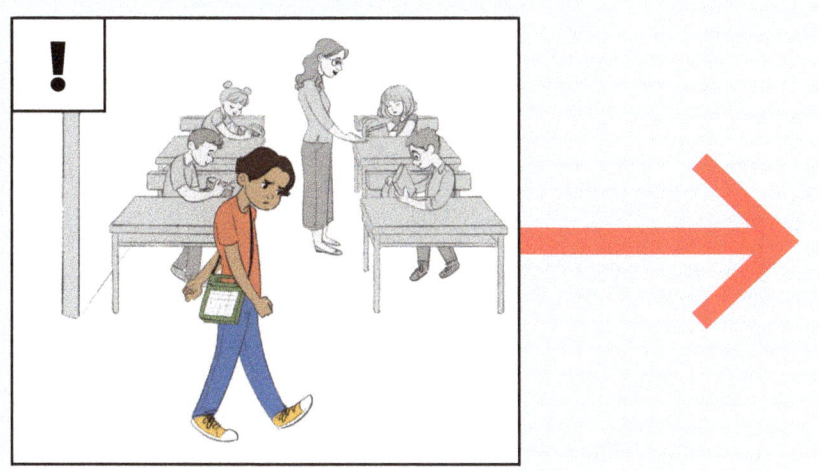

Missed opportunity

No response or challenging behaviors may occur.

Go to page 88

Legend

▪ Vocal	**Bold text:** Core words	
▪ ASL		
▪ AAC device & Core board	Standard text: Fringe words	

Social Self-Advocacy

Goal

Have a plan for getting out of an uncomfortable social situation.

How

Unfortunately, some learners may experience rude and disrespectful behavior directed towards them. It is important for AAC users to have a skillset in responding to these comments. When this situation arises, pause to give the AAC user an opportunity to self-advocate. If they do, assist them in resolving the situation or providing a safe space. If they do not, turn this into a learning opportunity through modeling (page 88).

Context

Responding to rude comments or bullies can include asking the person to leave them alone, moving to another seat, or asking a trusted adult for help. Try creating a visual of their self-advocacy options and placing this in an easy to access spot (see "Communication" illustration)!

Tip

It can be easy to jump in and support our AAC users during these uncomfortable moments. Instead, teach them through modeling how to advocate for their own needs so that they can independently manage these situations in the future. This is also a great opportunity to incorporate AAC to support when they are not comfortable vocally speaking out (refer to page 18 for augmentative vs. alternative).

Communication opportunity

An uncomfortable or disrespectful social situation.

Teaching targets

- stop
- go away
- please
- no
- don't want
- don't like
- help

Communication

AAC user independently self-advocates (e.g., "leave me alone," "stop," or asking a trusted adult for help).

Communication outcome

Assist in resolving the situation or providing a safe space.

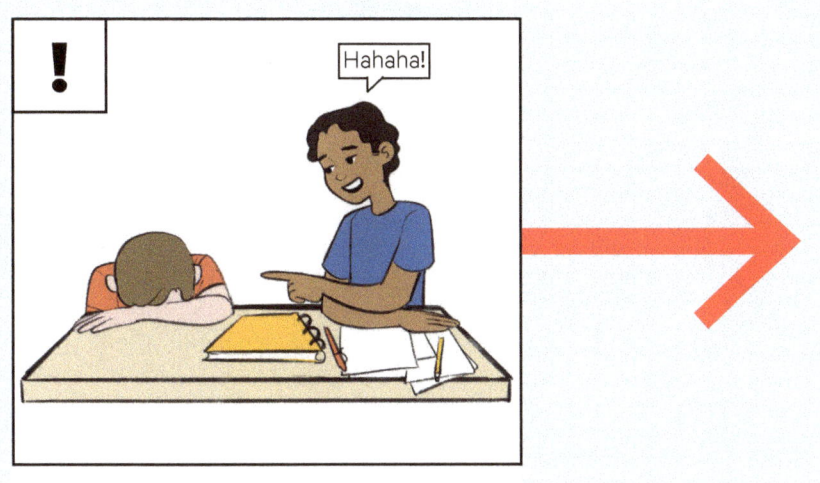

Missed opportunity

Uncomfortable situation continues or challenging behaviors may occur.

Go to page 88

Legend

- 🔲 Vocal
- 🟪 ASL
- 🟦 Texting

Bold text:
Core words

Standard text:
Fringe words

Health Check-in

Communication opportunity

Be on the lookout for signs of distress or discomfort. Ensure easy access to AAC.

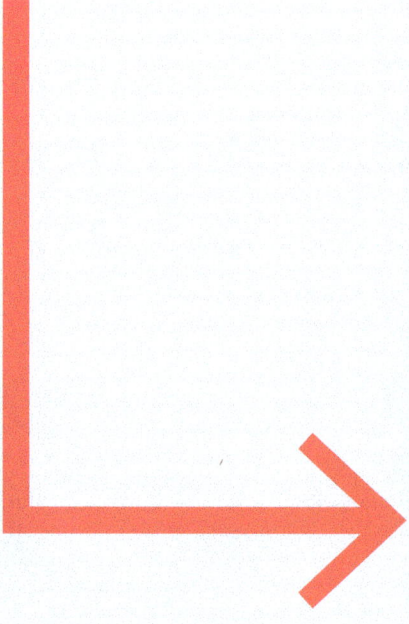

Goal

Identify & advocate for needs.

How

Ensure that AAC is available at all times so that when a need arises, the AAC user can effectively communicate their need. Using their preferred AAC system, ask if they need anything or are uncomfortable. Pause to give the AAC user an opportunity to independently respond. If they do, assist them with getting their needs met. If they do not, but clearly are in need, turn this into a learning opportunity through modeling (page 88). Note: if it's a medical emergency, just jump in and help.

Context

There are many occasions in which an AAC user would benefit from being able to express their health needs: if they are sick, did not sleep well, need a diaper change, or need medical assistance within a care facility, etc.

Tip

Choose an AAC system that is easy and quick to use, even if they have a repertoire of more expansive communication skills. In these moments, accept all forms of communication including gestures, pointing, and pantomiming to request basic health needs.

Teaching targets

- feel
- need
- want
- tell
- like / don't like

- help
- stop
- good / bad
- on / off
- up / down

Communication

AAC user independently identifies their health need.

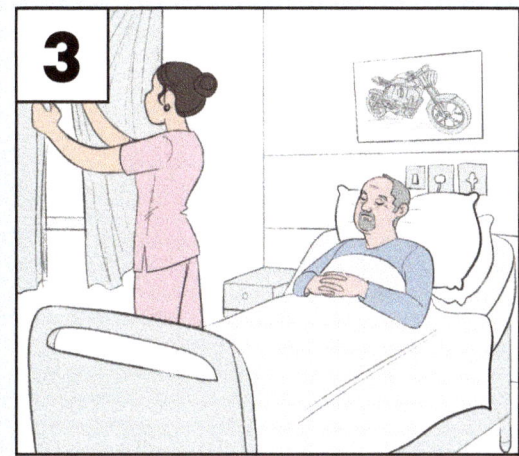

Communication outcome

Assist them with getting their needs met.

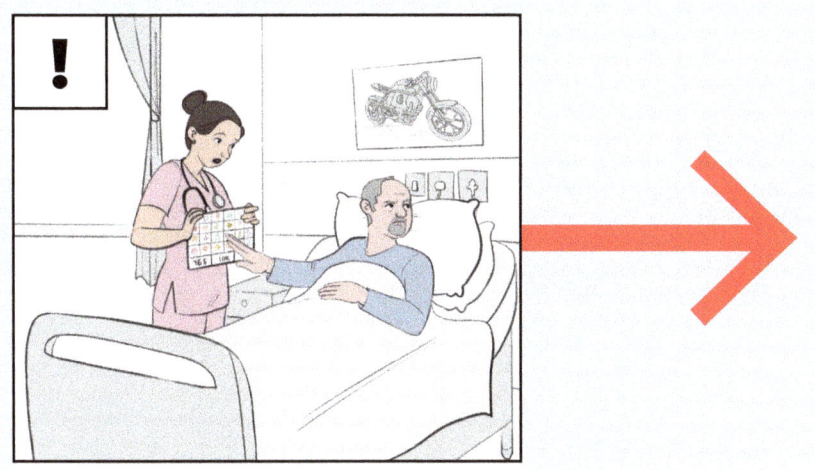

Missed opportunity

No response or challenging behaviors may occur. Note: if it's a medical emergency, just jump in and help.

Go to page 88

Legend

◥ Vocal

◼ ASL

◼ AAC device & Core board

Bold text:
Core words

Standard text:
Fringe words

Safety

Goal

Establish an understanding of what is and is not safe.

How

In new situations, help your learner communicate to you that they are unsure (teaching safety awareness). Provide clear feedback on if the situation is "safe" or "unsafe," explaining why. This helps establish a framework of what types of situations are safe/unsafe, building independence in this skill over time. After they have learned to ask about safety, shift your focus to rewarding safe decisions! Establish a specific reward they can earn for engaging in specific safe behaviors.

Context

Role play in a safe area to proactively teach safe/unsafe scenarios in order to prepare them for real-life situations. For example, going to a new place with family (safe), seeing a stranger at the park (unsafe), staying in the classroom (safe), running away from the teacher (unsafe), or holding hands while crossing the street (safe).

Tip

To start, try teaching versatile safety words/phrases using AAC such as "stranger," "I need to call my mom," or "go away," and then expanding to add more context-specific language.

A new person, setting, or event

When there's a new experience, teach learners to turn towards trusted adults to find out more.

Communication opportunity

AAC user communicates that they are unsure about this new experience (e.g., "Is this ok?" "Is this safe?").

Communication outcome: Not safe

Using their same AAC method, communicate that the situation is not safe, and explain why.

Support in safety

Lead the learner to an area or activity that is safe. This establishes that when they ask you for help, you can help guide them.

Teaching targets
- who
- can
- help
- know

Communication outcome: Safe

Using their same AAC method, communicate that the situation is safe and explain why.

Support in learning

In order to establish safety skills, communicate why this new experience is safe.

Autonomy

Goal

Promote self-advocacy through expressing perspective.

How

Throughout the day, questions/tasks may be asked of the AAC user. During these moments, give the AAC user an opportunity to express their own perspective. If they communicate their preference in that moment, validate it whenever possible and honor it. If they do not and the situation escalates, turn this into a learning opportunity through modeling (page 88).

Context

Autonomy means the right to make your own decision. Depending on the AAC user's age, there are differing ranges in how much autonomy they have. Try to honor these requests as much as possible so that we are teaching that essential phrases like "I don't want to" and "I don't like that" have value.

Tip

This is where flexibility comes in! There are times that an instruction has to be followed (e.g., going to school in the morning, brushing teeth, etc). Consider if this task can be delayed or made easier somehow following the AAC user's expression of feelings.

Communication opportunity

A task or activity is presented.

Teaching targets

- I/me/my
- like / don't like
- now / not now
- no thank you

Communication

AAC user expresses disinterest. At first, teach a script like "I don't want to." Then, expand language to provide the rationale.

Communication outcome

Validate their feelings, and whenever possible, honor their request. It's all about flexibility!

Missed opportunity

No response or challenging behaviors may occur.

Go to page 88

Legend

🖤 Vocal		**Bold text:** Core words
💗 ASL		
💙 AAC device & Core board		Standard text: Fringe words

Expressing & Managing Emotions

Goal

Learn to label & address emotional needs.

How

Establish a routine for checking in about emotions. This helps to normalize all feelings, rather than only focusing on feelings when they are negative. Throughout the day, model how you are feeling too! ("I'm feeling happy; I'd love to keep playing with you!" or "I'm feeling stressed; I'm going to take a break by myself.") For many learners, visuals are very helpful for this particular concept. Based on how your learner responds, support them in getting their needs met.

Context

Identify different activities that can promote coping and self-regulation skills. Try setting up a "Calm Corner" in your home or classroom that has a variety of items/ activities that learners can use independently (i.e., guided breathing posters, sensory toys, blankets, etc). Normalize using the Calm Corner for a range of emotions, not just anger.

Tip

Communicate about all emotions equally! On an AAC Device, use the "Feelings" folder to ask your AAC user how they are feeling. It's a built-in visual!

Plan

Establish a routine for checking in about emotions. This could be at the start of the school day or session, or when they get home from school.

Communication opportunity

Ask the learner how they are feeling, preferably using their AAC method.

Communication

If they respond that they are happy, excited, calm, etc, validate their communication by saying, "I'm happy to hear that!"

Communication outcome

They have shared with you that they are ready to participate!

Legend

- 🗨 Vocal
- 🗨 ASL
- 🗨 AAC device & Core board

Bold text:
Core words

Standard text:
Fringe words

Teaching targets

- I/me/my
- need
- want
- feel
- go
- help

Communication

If they respond that they are tired, angry, frustrated, anxious, etc, validate their communication by supporting them in choosing a coping skill.

Communication outcome

By establishing communication about how they are feeling and then taking care of those needs, you are teaching emotional regulation skills (i.e., when I feel ___, I can ___).

Following Directions

Opportunity

Recognize an upcoming instruction that may be tricky for your learner.

Goal

Increase success with instructions.

How

When you are giving vocal instructions, use AAC as a visual support to make the instructions even more clear! If they follow the instruction, make sure to recognize & celebrate this success. If they do not, try showing flexibility within your instruction by offering task-related choices or offering to get started with them (ABA terminology: behavior momentum).

Context

For instructions that are typically tricky, learners may more easily comprehend and respond if you use multimodal communication (vocal + visual). Here, there is no communication expectation from them, just them following through on the instruction!

Tip

When there is an instruction that your learner has a hard time following, try making this instruction easier for them by giving them a heads-up of what is to come (ABA terminology: priming with AAC) or getting their input on how to do the task (ABA terminology: providing choices with AAC).

Legend

 Vocal

ASL

AAC device & Core board

Bold text:
Core words

Standard text:
Fringe words

Teaching targets

- you do
- we do
- go / stop
- open / close
- get

- come
- make
- let's
- work
- this / that

Instruction

Get in close proximity and use their AAC method to provide a clear instruction.

Reward

Celebrate the success! Try establishing this reward ahead of time to make following directions even more motivating.

Firm, but flexible

If no response or challenging behaviors occur, repeat the instruction but now include a choice.

Frequently Asked Questions

Q: What should I do if the AAC user is stimming with the device (repeatedly pressing particular icons while not communicating to anyone)?

A: Stimming can sometimes be seen as not using AAC purposefully or functionally. However, there is a reason this communication is happening; we just may not be sure what that is. Regardless of why, do not take their communication device away! Instead, focus on building other types of communication skills and emphasizing the social connection aspects of communication. Here are some "stimming" behaviors specific to AAC:

- Exploring/Babbling: Are the hits random without a pattern and off-topic? Is the device new? Is the activity new? The AAC user may be exploring and babbling just like infants do with vocal sounds! They are exploring the meanings and what those symbols sound like to understand their context within their environment. It's normal, expected, and ok!
- Specific/Preferred Vocabulary: Does the AAC user really like certain words? Do they go to a page or word that seems off-topic a lot? They may love this word for what it gets them, or they may love the sound of it or the picture. We all have our favorites. We want to honor this. It is ok!
- Echolalia/Scripting: Some AAC users may engage in scripting as they learn AAC; this is ok! As they learn more and more ways to communicate, they will develop more ways to use their AAC system functionally. This AAC user may be a gestalt language processor—read more about this on page 34.
- Self-Regulation/Coping: There are times when an AAC user is truly dysregulated and using the device to help with that. This is ok! Imagine a time you felt anxious, nervous, or angry—if someone removed a coping strategy you had, how would you feel? We want to try to understand their regulation strategies to support the AAC user (vs. removing the system at this moment). We can also offer other coping supports if they appear in distress.

Q: What should I do when they are not navigating the screen effectively?

A: Take a moment to reflect on how your AAC user learns the quickest with the least amount of frustration. They may need a little extra teaching! Prompting and reinforcement are effective ways of teaching new skills. In prompting, you assist the AAC user with navigating their system by modeling or pointing. We don't want to stick around in this phase too long, as they may learn to become dependent on our support. Gradually pull back the assistance you're providing to give them opportunities to try on their own. With reinforcement, we want to recognize and reward every occurrence of using their AAC correctly! This will keep the motivation high to continue navigating effectively and independently.

Q: What should I do if they are editing the buttons on their own?

A: This is a good thing! This is an "operational competency of AAC," meaning how independent an AAC user is with their system. For example, an AAC user may learn to power on and off their device, control the volume, navigate the pages, and make custom edits. However, if an AAC user often accidentally gets into the app and deletes, adds, moves, hides, or rearranges symbols, consider using built-in features like "parental controls" and "guided access" or requiring a password before editing. You can also use built-in backups in case an AAC user unintentionally edits their device so that you can revert to the last backup in their system.

Q: What if they respond "wrong"? For example, you ask, "How are you feeling?" when they are crying, but they point to "happy" on their core board.

A: AAC users shouldn't need to be afraid of being wrong. They need to feel supported in making mistakes to learn the power of communication, and all their language offers them. Communication partners should acknowledge and shape communication attempts. Just as we can never assume what a speaking individual may say, we can not presume what an AAC user has to say. Validate their communication, then ask for clarification. For example, "You said you feel happy, but I see that you're crying. I think you might also be feeling sad (model sad), is that right?"

Templates & Tools

Introduction

The following pages contain a collection of templates, tools, and resources to assist you in introducing and implementing AAC. We have designed these to be used alongside the skills taught in this book to help promote more effective use of AAC. Feel free to make copies to share with your collaborative team!

Below, we've organized the tools and templates by their intended goal.

Introducing AAC

- WOW and ACE Planning Forms (blank & samples)
- Core Words
- Core Board

Creating a collaborative team

- Collaboration Plan
- Tips for Collaboration
- Skills Checklist

Training your team

- Sample Goals
- Datasheet

WOW Planning Form

A plan for introducing communication

Goal

Provide a structured approach to teaching new words.

How

Each week, choose your target word(s) such as a core word, a set of opposites, or a gestalt (a commonly "chunked" phrase) to focus on. Write your WOW in the center of the form. Write words/phrases you can model using your WOW in each of the settings/contexts. Use Teaching: WOW (page 72) to model language every day. Prior to each activity, reference your planning form as a reminder of how you can incorporate the WOW during this time. Speak in full sentences, but model the WOW using AAC.

Context

Be a team leader! Place planning form where it will be easily seen as a reminder of the core word of the week + share this plan with all team members to try to reach the 100x per day goal. Add sentence: We created two samples on the next page to get you started!

Tip

Core words accumulate! Each week, when filling out the form, try to use past WOW and current WOW in your words/phrases. For teachers: try putting all the WOW words on a word wall in your classroom.

Tips for using a WOW Planning Form

When choosing your first Word(s) of the Week, consider words that can easily and frequently be used across different activities such as "like," "go," or "open."

For early learners, try choosing opposites like "up/down," "on/off," "stop/go," as these have a natural cause and effect that helps teach communication in context.

Gestalt language processors may benefit from choosing a whole phrase as the WOW such as "I'll be back," "I love it!" or "Let's go."

Your collaborative team can help you choose which target words would be best for your learner. Take a few minutes to fill out the planning form with your ideas on how to incorporate the WOW throughout daily activities.

Print and post the planning form near where these activities take place so that all team members can use as a quick reference to know what communication to model during each activity.

WOW Planning

For core word of the week

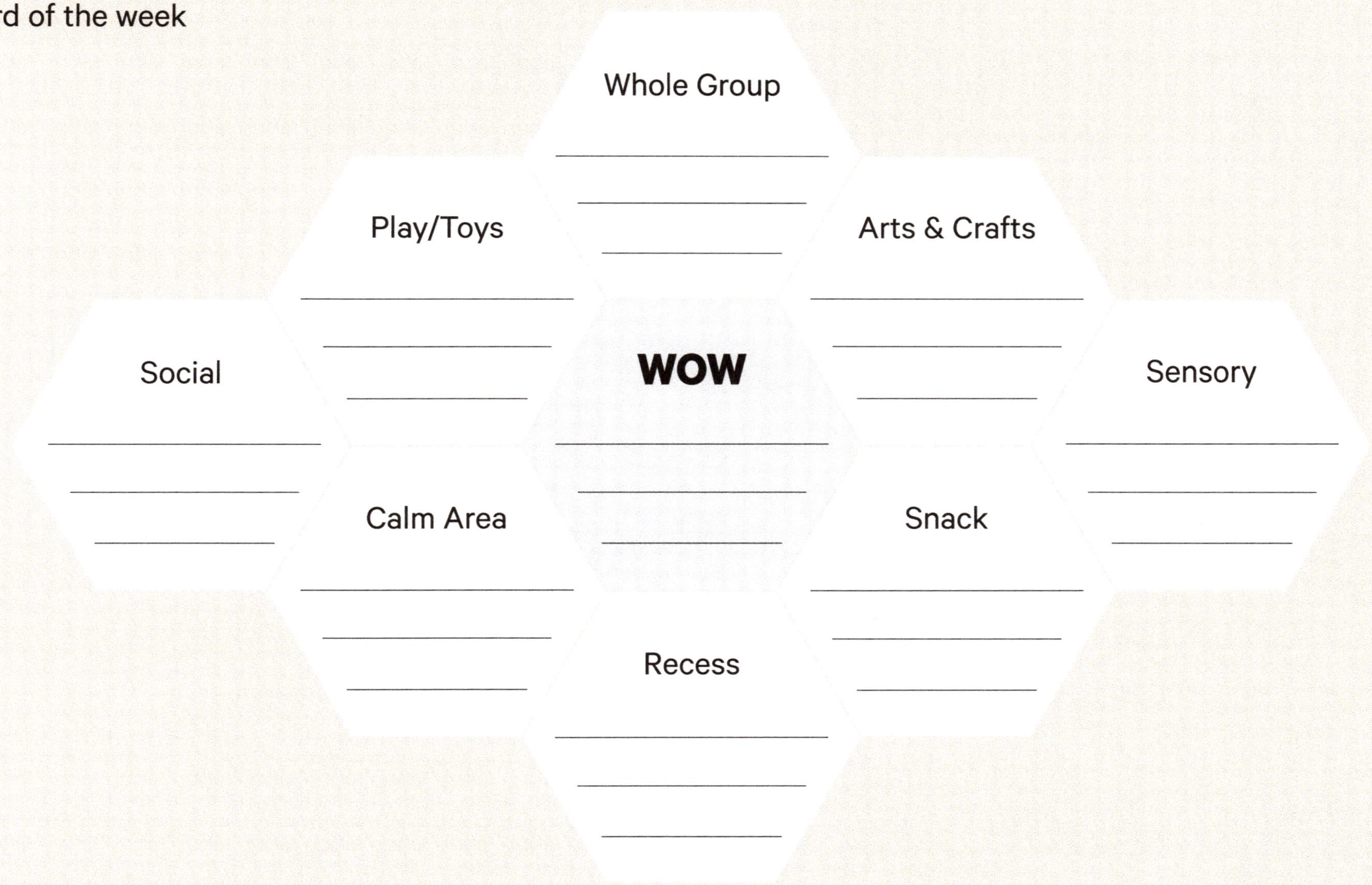

Social

Play/Toys

Calm Area

Whole Group

WOW

Recess

Arts & Crafts

Snack

Sensory

After choosing your WOW, determine the phrase that you will model in each activity!

WOW Planning

For core word of the week

WOW

Let's go ___

Whole Group

Let's go sing! ___

Let's go sit ___

Play/Toys

Let's go fast! ___

Let's go now ___

Social

Let's go play! ___

Let's go together! ___

Calm Area

Let's go to calm corner ___

Let's go to lie down ___

Recess

Let's go line up ___

Let's go down the slide! ___

Arts & Crafts

Let's go wash hands ___

Let's go paint ___

Snack

Let's go eat! ___

Let's go throw away ___

Sensory

Let's go jump! ___

Let's go swing! ___

After choosing your WOW, determine the phrase that you will model in each activity!

WOW Planning

For core word of the week

Social
same shoes
different shoes
___

Play/Toys
same cars
different toy
___

Calm Area
same squishy
different bean bag
___

Whole Group
same book/story
different helper
___

WOW
same
different
___

Recess
same friend
different ball
___

Arts & Crafts
same color
different paper
___

Snack
same snack
different drink
___

Sensory
same one
different choice
___

After choosing your WOW, determine the phrase that you will model in each activity!

ACE Planning Form

A plan for expanding communication

Goal

Provide a structured approach to teaching the expansiveness of communication.

How

Each day, choose one activity and write it in the center. Write words/phrases you can model during this activity for each communication reason (e.g., comments, rejections, continuations, expressing emotions). During the activity, use this guide to lead your communication by modeling the planned phrases using AAC (see Teaching: ACE page 76).

Context

Be a team leader! Collaboratively create your plan, then share it with the team so that everyone can model communication during the specific activity. We created two samples on the next page to get you started!

Tip

Choose activities that the AAC user already enjoys to increase interest and motivation. For teachers: start with structured whole group activities like circle time or morning meetings.

Tips for using an ACE Planning Form

Use activities that your AAC learner already loves! Remember, this form is all about modeling. So when selecting targets, keep in mind things that your AAC user may say about the activity, for example, "**Let's play again**!" or "**This is** fun! **I like** it!"

In the teaching phase, there is no expectation for your AAC learner to copy what you are modeling or respond with AAC. You are teaching them their language by modeling the words/phrases from your ACE Planning Form.

The ACE + Pause phase is where you are creating communication opportunities (page 78). Here is your AAC learner's opportunity to respond in their preferred mode. Your AAC learner has the right to respond with anything they want to "say," even if it is not on your planning form. That is the power of having a voice!

If they don't respond, just keep modeling.

If they respond with something that does not quite fit, repeat and validate what they said, and then keep modeling! If they make a request that you are not able to fulfill, it is okay to tell your AAC user, "no," "not right now," or "not yet," just as you would with any other student or individual. Bonus points for using AAC to say, "no."

ACE Planning

For activities

Placing words
(up, down, in, out)

Verbs related
to the activity

Prepositions

Fringe
Words

Pronouns

ACTIVITY

Words to ask
for continuation

Words to
express emotion

Comments

Words to
end or reject

Specific words/nouns related to
this activity (not from core list)

Prioritize making
comments over asking
questions

Try starting with I,
me, or you!

Choose a preferred activity and use this planning
form to ensure you are expanding communication.

ACE Planning

For activities

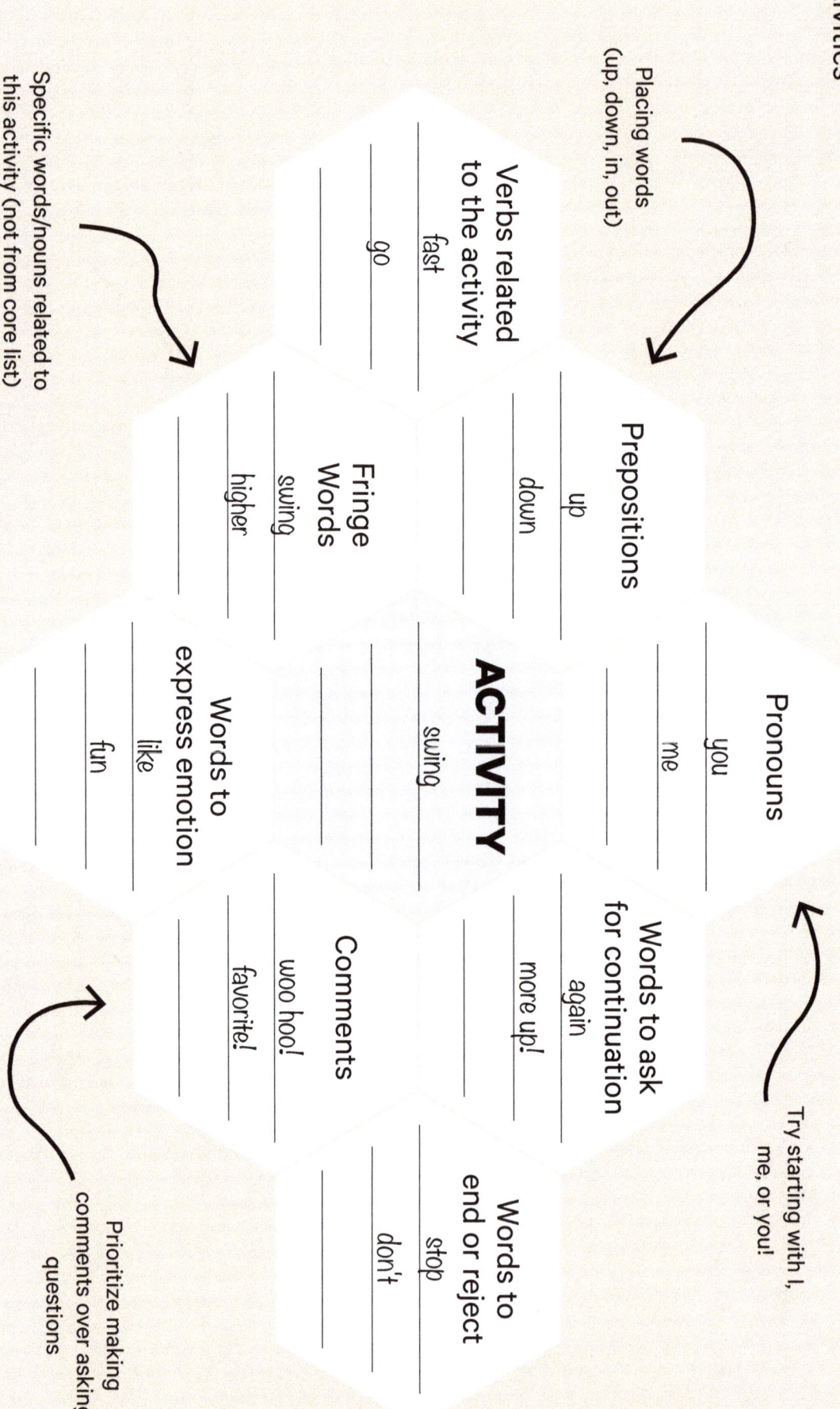

Placing words
(up, down, in, out)

**Verbs related
to the activity**

fast

go

Prepositions

up

down

you

me

Pronouns

**Fringe
Words**

swing

higher

ACTIVITY

swing

**Words to ask
for continuation**

again

more up!

**Words to
express emotion**

like

fun

Comments

woo hoo!

favorite!

**Words to
end or reject**

stop

don't

Specific words/nouns related to
this activity (not from core list)

Try starting with I,
me, or you!

Prioritize making
comments over asking
questions

Choose a preferred activity and use this planning
form to ensure you are expanding communication.

ACE Planning

For activities

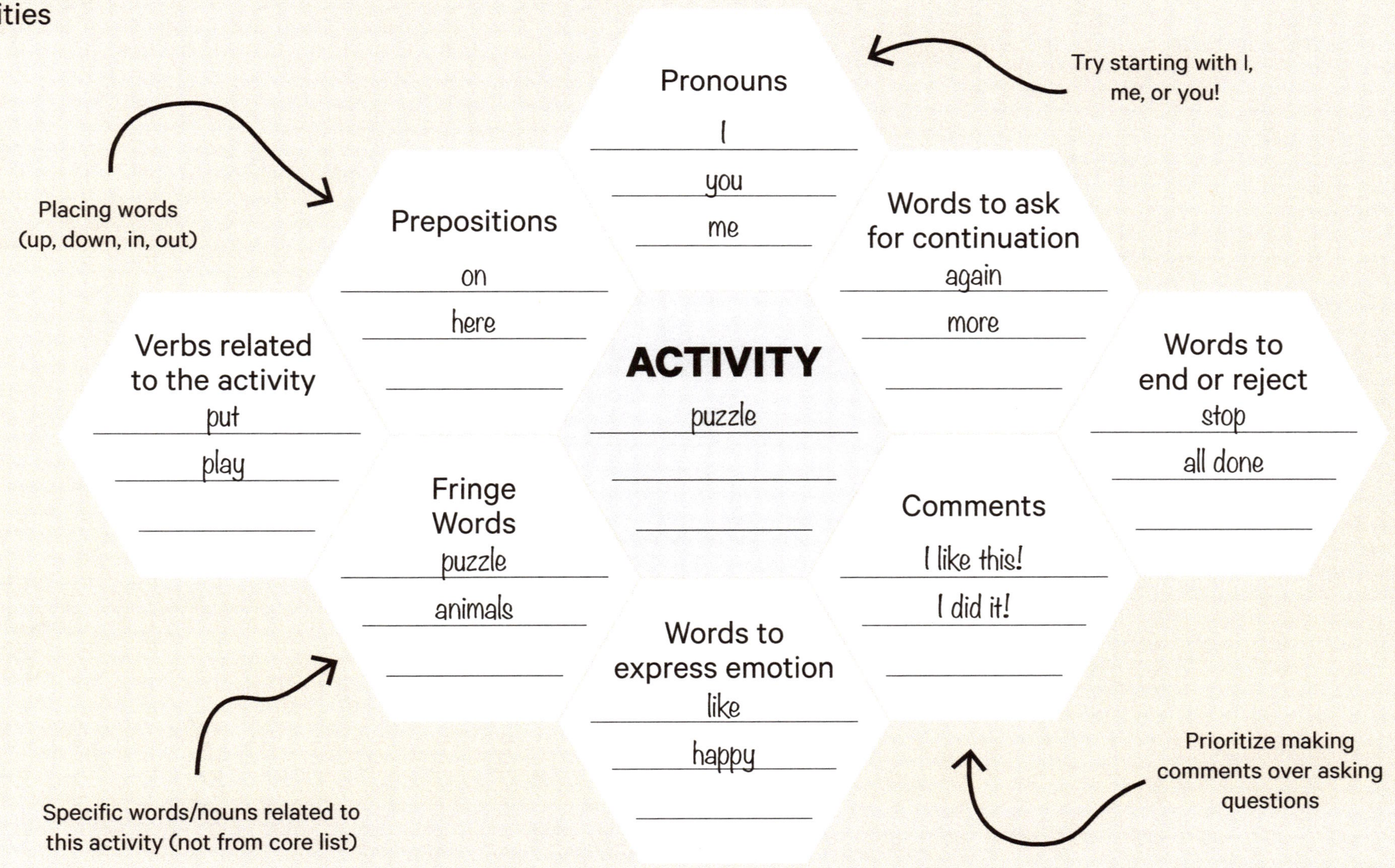

Placing words
(up, down, in, out)

Verbs related to the activity

put
_____
_____
play
_____

Prepositions

on
_____
_____
here
_____
me

Fringe Words

puzzle
_____
_____
animals
_____

ACTIVITY

puzzle
_____

Pronouns

I
_____
you
_____
_____

Words to ask for continuation

again
_____
_____
more
_____

Words to express emotion

like
_____
_____
happy
_____

Comments

I like this!
_____
_____
I did it!
_____

Words to end or reject

stop
_____
_____
all done
_____

Try starting with I, me, or you!

Specific words/nouns related to this activity (not from core list)

Prioritize making comments over asking questions

Choose a preferred activity and use this planning form to ensure you are expanding communication.

137

Core Words List

Top 100 words!

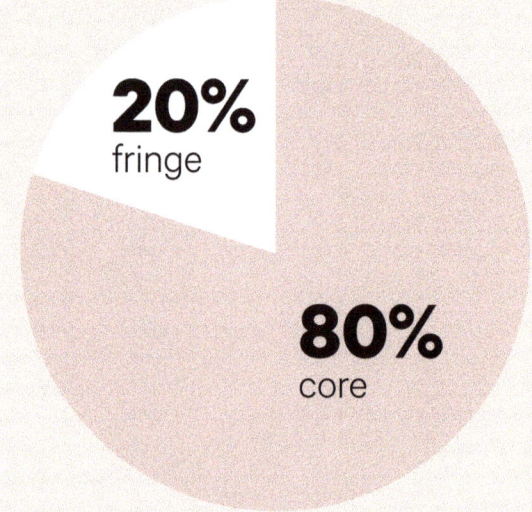

20%
fringe

80%
core

Goal

Familiarize yourself with core words.

How

Make a copy of this page so that you can reference it often. The aim is to use as many core words as possible when teaching AAC. To use in alignment with WOW, highlight core words that have already been introduced.

Context

These 100 words are common first words to prioritize with new AAC learners. You may notice that they align with high-frequency sight words that students learn to read first!

Tip

Try to rephrase instructions and comments replacing fringe words with core words when possible. This might take a little practice and creativity!

The power of core!

It may be tricky to focus on core words because they are not as visual or descriptive as fringe words. However, if we teach core words, our learners can use language in much wider contexts, truly expanding their communication use. For example, if we teach the fringe word "cookie," they can only request and label. If we teach the core word "eat," we can talk about eating at different times of the day, ask questions about eating and mealtimes, and share food preferences. Core = more!

Social words
(Interjections)

- yes
- no
- thank you
- please
- hi/hello
- goodbye

Pronouns

- I
- me
- my
- mine
- you
- it
- he
- she
- we
- they

Question words

- what
- when
- where
- who
- why
- how

Helping words
(Preverbs)

- be
- is
- am
- are
- was
- were
- do
- did
- can
- have
- will

Action words
(Verbs)

- go
- stop
- turn
- make
- look
- see
- find
- put
- open
- close
- eat
- drink
- get
- help
- want
- need
- say
- tell
- come
- read
- like
- feel
- color
- let's
- work
- play
- finished/all done

Words that tell when,
where, how (Adverbs)

- not/don't
- now
- here
- there
- away
- again

Connecting words
(Conjunctions)

- and
- but

Placing words
(Prepositions)

- on
- off
- in
- out
- up
- down
- to
- for
- under
- with

Pointer words
(Determiners)

- this
- that
- some
- all

Descriptive words
(Adjectives)

- more
- one
- big
- little
- fast
- slow
- same
- different
- pretty
- red
- blue
- yellow
- good
- bad
- new
- old
- happy
- sad

Core Board

Making language visual & accessible

Goal

Provide quick, easy access to AAC.

How

Make a copy and laminate it for durability. Bring the core board everywhere! Use it as a modeling tool to "point and say" communication throughout the day. For learners who are on Teaching Plus or Independence, they can communicate with the core board as well.

Context

While you are waiting for your individualized AAC assessment results, use a core board to start introducing common words and provide your learner with an effective means of communication. For teachers: try placing these all around the classroom to promote even more access to communication opportunities!

Tip

If the AAC user's device is misplaced or the battery is dead, use a core board in the meantime to continue providing access to communication. Take a screenshot of their device homescreen to have a core board that is individualized for them!

Tips for using a core board

- Use "point and say."
- Highlight or circle the WOW.
- If all the icons are too overwhelming, try making a black and white copy and color in a few words that you'd like to focus on.
- Print multiple copies and laminate them.
- If you're worried about a device getting wet (e.g., pool, beach, water play), use a core board during that activity instead.
- For teachers: put a printed core board and a printed planning form back to back in a sheet protector so that everything you need is all together in one place!

I	you	hi	bye	yes	no
want	go	look	make	like	not
get	stop	buy	come	have	play
more	this	that	eat	drink	help
what	who	where	in	big	all done
again	all	some	out	small	thank you

141

Collaboration Plan

Be a leader for your AAC user

Goal

Increase success through teamwork.

How

Set up a meeting with everyone involved in the AAC user's communication plan: family, teachers, and providers. This meeting can be virtual! Establish what communication skills the team is prioritizing and how these skills should be taught. Share the completed plan with everyone on the team and determine a follow-up meeting date to promote accountability.

Context

Every AAC user should have a collaboration plan! Whatever role you have in your AAC user's life, we encourage you to be a leader in establishing this team. Refer to roles starting on page 38. More teamwork = more success!

Tip

Collaboration is essential! Start with identifying a shared goal. Listen to others' ideas on how to reach this goal, be flexible in your recommendations, and focus on your shared love for your learner.

Instructions

Phase

Write which phase you're currently in

- Teaching
- Teaching Plus
- Independent

Set up

How will the team create a learning opportunity?

AAC user's role

What is the AAC user's expected role at this time?

Response

How will you respond?

Adaptability

Make it work for you! Describe how this skill could be taught in your setting.

- Home:
- School:
- Therapy:

Accountability

Write your agreed-upon next meeting date to review progress.

Template

AAC User _____

Shared Goal _____

Phase	Set up	AAC user's role	Response	Adaptability	Accountability

Sample

AAC User _____ TaBe

Shared Goal _____ Use 1+ word to reject

Phase	Set up	AAC user's role	Response	Adaptability	Accountability
Teaching	Team member offers a nonpreferred item	AAC user watches while team member models "don't like," "no," or "stop" using AAC	Team member teaches the power of communication by removing the nonpreferred item	Home: peas School: writing Therapy: slime	July 16, 2023
Teaching Plus	Team member offers a nonpreferred item + pause	AAC user watches while team member models "don't like," "no," or "stop" using AAC + possibly copies the phrase OR "no" "don't like" "stop"	Team member teaches the power of communication by removing the nonpreferred item	Home: peas School: writing Therapy: slime	August 1, 2023
Independent	Team member offers a nonpreferred item	AAC user communicates "don't like," "no," or "stop"	Team member honors their communication by removing the nonpreferred item	Home: peas School: writing Therapy: slime	August 25, 2023

Tips for Collaboration

Establish a respectful, collaborative tone

Goal

Provide scripts that promote respectful collaboration.

How

Think back to times that you've had great collaborative experiences and not so great ones. What were the differences in those conversations? We've outlined some dos and don'ts to get you started!

Context

Anyone can be the leader of the collaborative team! Use these recommended phrases to help guide a humble and productive conversation.

Tip

Nervous about your upcoming collaboration meeting? Write a few prepared questions or respectful phrases in your notebook to refer back to when needed.

Instead of...

- Assuming you understand their expertise and perspective based on their credentialing
- Giving feedback and recommendations right away
- Asking yes/no questions that may come off judgmental, such as "do you know about...," or "have you tried..."
- Trusting that because you are using evidence-based practices within your field, they ensure effective progress

Try this!

- Start the conversation with "I'd love to know more about your specific areas of expertise and interests within (field)"
- Listen first!
- Ask open-ended questions like "Tell me about what you've already tried," or "What topics would you like to prioritize we talk about today?"
- Sharing ideas with "This reminds me of..."
- Make sure that your practices align with all other team members. Cohesive strategies lead to the best results!

SLP

Teacher

Paraprofessional

ABA provider

Occupational Therapist (OT)

Teacher

Paraprofessional

Skills Checklist

Let's check in!

Goal

Determine skill level at any point in time.

How

At the start of your AAC collaboration, work with the team to determine which skills the AAC user is already doing independently and check those off. The remainder may be good choices for skill-building targets!

Context

Return back to this checklist with the whole team as a way to systematically check in on the AAC user's overall communication development.

Tip

With support of the BCBA and SLP on your team, use this checklist in conjunction with actual direct assessments for most accurate reflection of skill level.

Understanding communication competencies

One of the most important things to remember about AAC is that it can be used in many different situations and for various reasons. The AAC competencies listed on this page can be worked on or learned simultaneously because many of the competencies can be interwoven. For example, asking questions can be both social and linguistic. Your AAC user is learning to combine words into sentences and use language to initiate, interact, and maintain conversations with their communication partners.

SLP terminology: Operational competencies

Skills specific for speech-generating devices

- ☐ Powers device on/off
- ☐ Independently navigates
- ☐ Adjusts volume
- ☐ Changes the brightness of the screen
- ☐ Adds or edits vocabulary
- ☐ Changes voice to reflect tone/mood
- ☐ Charges device
- ☐ Unlocks device
- ☐ Activates the message window
- ☐ Opens device stand
- ☐ Transports device

Communication competency

Communication skill

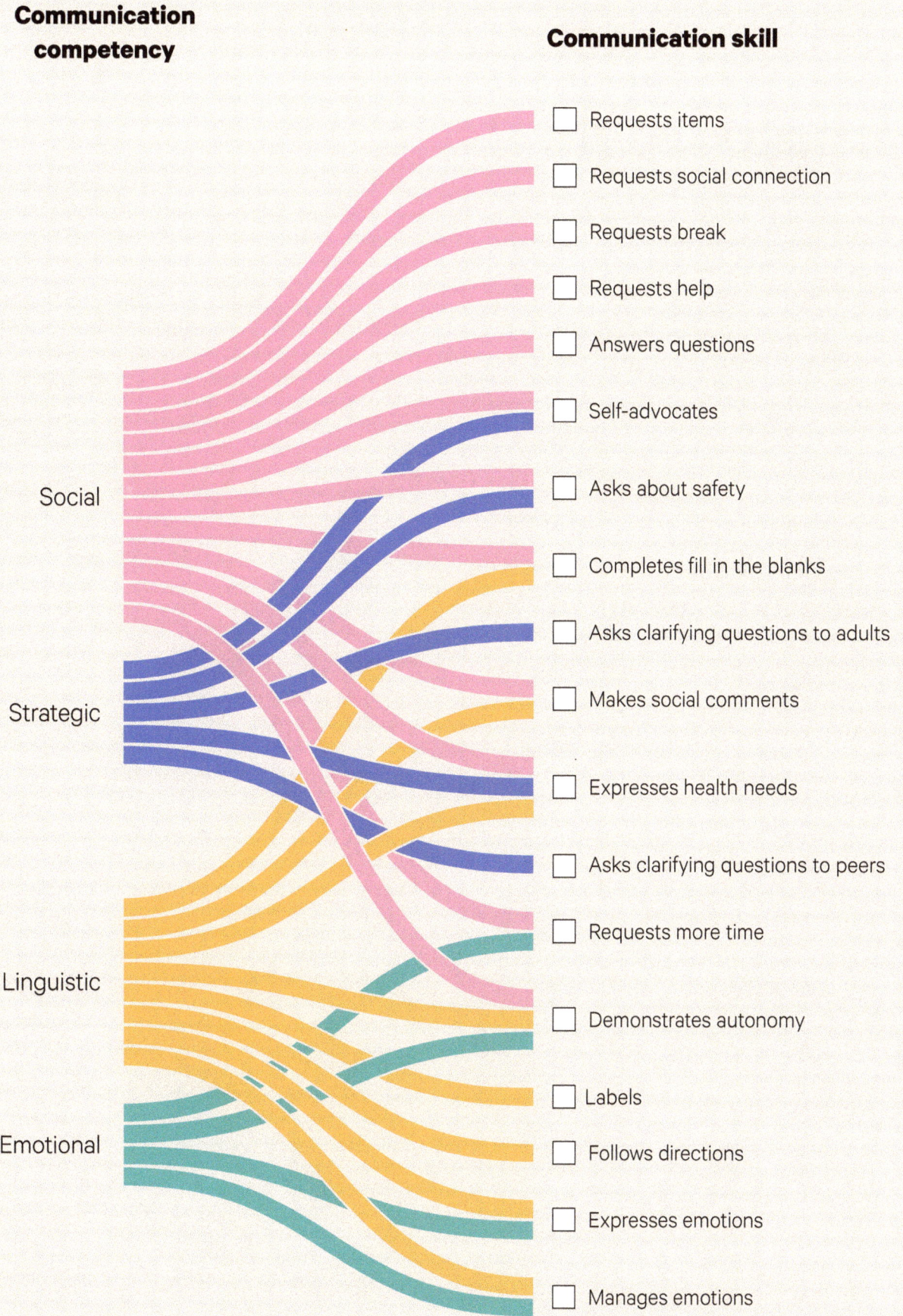

- [ ] Requests items
- [ ] Requests social connection
- [ ] Requests break
- [ ] Requests help
- [ ] Answers questions
- [ ] Self-advocates
- [ ] Asks about safety
- [ ] Completes fill in the blanks
- [ ] Asks clarifying questions to adults
- [ ] Makes social comments
- [ ] Expresses health needs
- [ ] Asks clarifying questions to peers
- [ ] Requests more time
- [ ] Demonstrates autonomy
- [ ] Labels
- [ ] Follows directions
- [ ] Expresses emotions
- [ ] Manages emotions

Social

Strategic

Linguistic

Emotional

Sample Goals

Jumpstart your goal writing!

Goal

Create a structured, individualized approach to goal setting.

How

Through your collaborative meeting, determine which AAC skills to target. Start with the template goals provided, customize them to your learner's preferences and context (including individualized mastery criteria), then use the datasheet to monitor progress.

Context

These goals can be adapted as IEP goals, ABA goals, or SLP goals. They can be taught at the same time as other IEP, ABA, or speech goals. Remember to individualize!

Tip

Discuss with your collaborative team how many goals should be introduced at one time. This is different for every learner!

Skill: WOW/ACE Plus
Goal: Following a model of (target word or phrase) using (type of AAC), learner will use (type of AAC) to communicate a 1+ word comment/phrase.

Skill: Requesting items (phase 1)
Goal: When a preferred item (provide individualized examples) is in sight, but out of reach, learner will use (type of AAC) to request using 1+ word comment/phrase.

Skill: Requesting items (phase 2)
Goal: When a preferred item (provide individualized examples) is out of sight and there is motivation for that item, learner will use (type of AAC) to request using 1+ word comment/phrase.

Skill: Requesting social connection (phase 1)
Goal: When a peer or family member is available nearby, learner will use (type of AAC) to request specific social connection (provide individualized examples) using 1+ word comment/phrase.

Skill: Requesting social connection (phase 2)
Goal: When there is motivation for social connection from a peer or family member, learner will approach them and use (type of AAC) to request specific social connection (provide individualized examples) using 1+ word comment/phrase.

Skill: Requesting breaks
Goal: During challenging tasks/activities (provide individualized examples) or on a predetermined break schedule, learner will use (type of AAC) to request a break using 1+ word comment/phrase.

Skill: Requesting help (phase 1)
Goal: During times when assistance is needed (provide individualized examples), learner will use (type of AAC) to request a nearby trusted adult for help using 1+ word comment/phrase.

Skill: Requesting help (phase 2)
Goal: During times when assistance is needed (provide individualized examples), learner will use (type of AAC) to request a nearby trusted adult for help using 2+ word "help + (specific action)" phrase.

Skill: Requesting more time
Goal: When asked to end current activity, but not ready to transition yet, learner will use (type of AAC) to request more time using 1+ word comment/phrase.

Skill: Labeling
Goal: During preferred activities (provide individualized examples), when presented with a familiar item (provide individualized examples), learner will use (type of AAC) to label the item using 1+ word comment/phrase.

Skill: Fill in the blanks
Goal: While singing familiar songs with family (provide individualized examples), when family members sing using (type of AAC) the beginning of the phrase and then pause, learner will use (type of AAC) to complete the phrase.

Skill: Social commenting
Goal: While engaging in preferred activities with peers (provide individualized examples), and following a peer's play-related comment (provide individualized examples), learner will use (type of AAC) to respond with a similar comment using 3+ words (provide individualized examples).

Skill: Asking questions
Goal: When there is an unfamiliar or unclear situation, learner will use (type of AAC) to ask a trusted adult a "Wh-"question to gain information.

Skill: Asking questions with peers
Goal: When there is an unfamiliar or unclear situation, learner will use (type of AAC) to ask a trusted peer a "Wh-"question to gain information.

Skill: Answering questions
Goal: When asked a question, learner will use (type of AAC) to respond using 3+ words.

Skill: Self-advocacy
Goal: When in an uncomfortable social situation (provide individualized examples), learner will use (type of AAC) to self-advocate by either requesting for the nearby person to "stop" or will ask a trusted adult for help.

Skill: Health check-in
Goal: When asked to identify how they are feeling, learner will use (type of AAC) to label their current emotion or needs.

Skill: Safety (phase 1)
Goal: In an unfamiliar situation/setting or when nearby an unfamiliar person (provide individualized examples), learner will use (type of AAC) to ask a trusted adult if the situation is safe or unsafe.

Skill: Safety (phase 2)
Goal: Learner will demonstrate discrimination skills by independently identifying if a situation is safe or unsafe (provide individualized examples) and then responding accordingly (provide individualized examples).

Skill: Autonomy
Goal: When asked to do a task/instruction, but not ready to initiate it yet, learner will use (type of AAC) to politely reject the instruction (provide individualized examples).

Skill: Expressing emotions
Goal: When asked to identify how they are feeling, learner will use (type of AAC) to label their emotion.

Skill: Managing emotions
Goal: After independently identifying their emotion, learner will choose an activity or coping strategy that aligns with that emotion (provide individualized examples).

Skill: Following directions
Goal: When a parent or teacher uses (type of AAC) to give a 1-step instruction (provide individualized examples), learner will initiate the instruction within 10 seconds of being asked.

Datasheet

Track their growth!

Goal

Establish an easy way to measure progress.

How

Determine your AAC user's current phase of learning and using AAC. Fill out the target word/phrase or communication opportunity aligned with the target skill that the collaborative team is working towards.
The established data collector will record the AAC user's success with that skill each day.

Context

This tool was made with ABA providers, SLPs, and teachers in mind. Determine the AAC goal, collect data, and evaluate progress!

Tip

Some AAC devices have built-in history that you can review, or you can download other apps to electronically track the data for you.

Introducing AAC sample
Teaching plus

Target word/phrase: more time

-	-	+	+	-
+	+	-	+	+
+	+	+	+	-
-	+	+		

Percentage: 12/18 = 67%

Further expanding AAC sample

Communication opportunity: Transitioning off electronics

Target skill: Requesting more time

-	+	+	-	+
+	+	+		

Percentage: 6/8 = 75%

Introducing AAC

Phase 1: Teaching: no data, only teaching

Phase 2: Teaching Plus

Instructions: Score + if the learner uses AAC to communicate following your communication + pause OR if your AAC learner initiates communication on their own. Score - if the learner engages in challenging behaviors or does not respond. At the end of each day, count the number of + responses out of the total amount of communication opportunities to calculate the percentage that the learner had success with this skill that day!

Target word/phrase:

Percentage:

Further Expanding AAC

Phase 3: Independent

Instructions: Identify the communication opportunity for the target skill (e.g., difficult task presented, transition instruction, engaged with peers, etc). Score + if the learner engages in independent communication following the opportunity. Score - if the learner engages in challenging behaviors or does not respond. At the end of each day, count the number of + responses out of the total amount of communication opportunities to calculate the percentage that the learner had success with this skill that day!

Communication opportunity:

Target skill:

Percentage:

Resources

Recommended AAC Resources

Resources for d/Deaf & hard of hearing individuals

- Signs of Communication, LLC - ABA services for the Deaf community + monthly resources for families & professionals
- ASL at Home routine-based ASL curriculum
- American Society for Deaf Children
- LifePrint free ASL
- Kids Sign Playlist (YouTube)
- MyGo! (ASL interpretations of popular children's shows on YouTube)
- Gallaudet University
- Hands & Voices non-profit organization

Books

- Natural Language Acquisition on the Autism Spectrum
- Comprehensive Literacy for All: Teaching Students with Significant Disabilities to Read and Write
- AAC in the Schools: Best Practice for Intervention
- Practically Speaking Language, Literacy, and Academic Development for Students with AAC Needs
- Transition Strategies for Adolescents and Young Adults who Use AAC
- Augmentative and Alternative Communication, Supporting Children and Adults with Complex Communication Needs
- Communicative Competencies for Individuals who use AAC: from Research to Effective Practice
- AAC for All: Culturally and Linguistically Responsive Practice

Children & youth books

- I Talk in Different Ways
- AAC Rhyme Time
- How Katie Got a Voice
- Eddie the Elephant has Something to Say
- Something to Say about My Communication Device
- Lucas the Lion Loves the Tiny Talker
- Sara's Surprise
- Me and My AAC
- All are Welcome
- On Being Sarah
- Dancing Daisies
- Inside my Outside: An independent mind in a Dependent Body
- Let's Get Cooking! Visual Recipes

Facebook groups

- Ask Me, I'm an AAC User
- A Voice Discovered
- AAC: Alternative Awesome Communicators
- AAC and Literacy
- AAC Family Fun Page
- AAC Through Motivate, Model, and Get Out of the Way
- AAC Chicks
- Podcasts
- Talking with Tech
- Speechie Side Up
- The Autism Helper
- SLP Nerdcast
- Asha Voices
- AAC Tip Talks
- Two Sides of the Spectrum

Trainings & Resources

- Project Core
- AAC Language Lab
- The Center for AAC and Autism
- PRC Saltillo
- Tarn Heel Shared Reader & Reader
- AssistiveWare
- AAC Learning Journey
- Proloquo Coach
- Gail Van Tatenhove
- Tobii Dynavox
- PRC Implementation Training
- The AAC Coach
- Meaningful Speech
- AAC Ally
- PrAACtical AAC

YouTube

- The AAC Coach
- Rachel Madel SLP
- AssistiveWare
- Emily Diaz

References

AAC Language Lab. Retrieved August 1, 2022, from https://aaclanguagelab.com/

AssistiveWare - What will you say? Retrieved August 1, 2022, from https://www.assistiveware.com/

Bishop, S.K., Moore, J.W., Dart, E.H., Radley, K., Brewer, R., Barker, L.K., Quintero, L., Litten, S., Gilfeather, A., Newborne, B., Toche, C. (2020). Further investigation of increasing vocalizations of children with autism with a speech-generating device. Journal of Applied Behavior Analysis, 53(1), 475-483.

Blackstone, S.W. & Wilkins, D.P. (2009). Exploring the importance of emotional competence in children with complex communication needs. Perspectives on Augmentative and Alternative Communication, 18, 78-87.

Bowman, K.S., Suarez, V.D., Weiss, M.J. (2021). Standards for interprofessional collaboration in the treatment of individuals with autism. Behavior Analysis in Practice, 3;14(4), 1191-1208.

Byers-Heinlein, K., & Lew-Williams, C. (2013). Bilingualism in the early years: what the science says. LEARNing Landscapes, 7(1), 95–112. Leading English Education.

Carbone, V.J., Lewis, L., Sweeney-Kerwin, E.J., Dixon, J., Louden, R., & Quinn, S. (2006). A comparison of two approaches for teaching VB functions: total communication vs. vocal-alone. The Journal of Speech and Language Pathology – Applied Behavior Analysis, 1(3), 181–192.

Carbone, V.J., Sweeney-Kerwin, E.J., Attanasio, V., Kasper, T. (2010). Increasing the vocal responses of children with autism and developmental disabilities using manual sign mand training and prompt delay. Journal of Applied Behavior Analysis, 43(4):705-9.

Carnett, A., Ingvarsson, E.T., Bravo, A., Sigafoos, J. (2020). Teaching children with autism spectrum disorder to ask "where" questions using a speech-generating device. Journal of Applied Behavior Analysis, 53(3), 1383-1403.

Cook, J.L., House, M., Rapp, J.T., Burji, C., McHugh, C., Nuta, R. (2017). A simple intervention for stereotypical engagement with an augmentative alternative communicative device. Behavioral Interventions.

Donato, C., Spencer, E., & Arthur-Kelly, M. (2018). A critical synthesis of barriers and facilitators to the use of AAC by children with autism spectrum disorder and their communication partners. Perspectives on Augmentative and Alternative Communication, 34(3), 242–253. Informa UK Limited.

Drysdale, H., van der Meer, L. & Kagohara, D. (2015). Children with autism spectrum disorder from bilingual families: a systematic review. Journal of Autism and Developmental Disorders, 2, 26–38.

Flippin, M., Reszka, S., Watson, L.R. (2010). Effectiveness of the picture exchange communication system (PECS) on communication and speech for children with autism spectrum disorders: a meta-analysis. American Journal of Speech-Language Pathology, 19(2), 178-95.

Frea, W. D., Arnold, C. L., & Vittimberga, G. L. (2001). A demonstration of the effects of augmentative communication on the extreme aggressive behavior of a child with autism within an integrated preschool setting. Journal of Positive Behavior Interventions, 3(4), 194–198.

Ganz, J.B., Liew, J., Yllades, V., Liao, C., Luo, W., Hong, E., Yoro, A.J., Rodriguez, D., Clark, S., Stein, K., & Ura, S.K. (2022). Communication and affective synchrony between parents and their children with autism during a multimodal communication parent-coaching intervention. Child & Family Behavior Therapy, 44:2, 113-134.

Gevarter, C., O'Reilly, M.F., Kuhn, M., Mills, K., Ferguson, R., Watkins, L., Sigafoos, J., Lang, R., Rojeski, L., Lancioni, G.E. (2016). Increasing the vocalizations of individuals with autism during intervention with a speech-generating device. Journal of Applied Behavior Analysis, 49(1), 17-33.

Goodwyn, S.W., Acredolo, L.P. & Brown, C.A. (2000). Impact of symbolic gesturing on early language development. Journal of Nonverbal Behavior 24, 81–103.

Ingersoll, B. R. (2009). Teaching social communication. Journal of Positive Behavior Interventions.

Kahng, S.W., Hendrickson, D.J., Vu, C.P. (2020). Comparison of single and multiple functional communication training responses for the treatment of problem behavior. Journal of Applied Behavior Analysis, 33(3), 321-4.

Kent-Walsh, J., Murza, K.A., Malani, M.D., Binger, C. (2015). Effects of communication partner instruction on the communication of individuals using AAC: a meta-analysis. Augmentative and Alternative Communication, 31(4), 271-84.

Koenig, M., & Gerenser, J. (2006). SLP-ABA: Collaborating to support individuals with communication impairments.The Journal of Speech and Language Pathology – Applied Behavior Analysis, 1(1), 2–10.

Light, J.C., Beukelman, D.R., & Reichle, J. (2003). Communicative competence for individuals who use augmentative and alternative communication. Baltimore: Paul H. Brooks Publishing Co.

Light, J., McNaughton, D., Caron, J. (2019). New and emerging AAC technology supports for children with complex communication needs and their communication partners: State of the science and future research directions. Augmentative and Alternative Communication, 35(1):26-41.

Logan, K., Iacono, T., & Trembath, D. (2016). A systematic review of research into aided AAC to increase social-communication functions in children with autism spectrum disorder. Augmentative and Alternative Communication, 33(1), 51–64.

Marya, V., Frampton, S., Shillingsburg, A. (2021). Matrix training to teach tacts using speech generating devices: Replication and extension. Journal of Applied Behavior Analysis, 54(3).

Millar, D.C., Light, J.C., Schlosser, R.W. (2006). The impact of augmentative and alternative communication intervention on the speech production of individuals with developmental disabilities: a research review. Journal of Speech, Language, and Hearing Research, 49(2), 248-64.

Pennington, R.C., Ault, M.J., Schmuck, D.G., Burt, J.L., Ferguson, L.L. (2015). Frequency of mand instruction reported in behavioral, special education, and speech journals. Behavior Analysis in Practice, 9(3), 235-42.

Reichle, J., Simacek, J., Wattanawongwan, S., Ganz, J. (2019). Implementing aided augmentative communication systems with persons having complex communicative needs. Behavior Modification, 43(6), 841-878.

Rodriguez, N.M., Levesque, M.A., Cohrs, V.L., Niemeier, J.J. (2017). Teaching children with autism to request help with difficult tasks. Journal of Applied Behavior Analysis, 0(4), 717-732.

Rose, V., Paynter, J., Vivanti, G., Keen, D., Trembath, D.. (2020). Predictors of expressive language change for children with autism spectrum disorder receiving AAC-infused comprehensive intervention. Journal of Autism and Developmental Disorders, 50(1), 278-291.

Shillingsburg, M.A., Marya, V., Bartlett, B.L., Thompson, T.M. (2019). Teaching mands for information using speech generating devices: A replication and extension. Journal of Applied Behavior Analysis, 52(3), 756-771.

Smith, A. L., Barton-Hulsey, A., & Nwosu, N. (2016). AAC and families: dispelling myths and empowering families. Augmentative and Alternative Communication, 1(12), 10-20.

Thiemann-Bourque, K., Brady, N., McGuff, S., Stump, K., & Naylor, A. (2016). Picture exchange communication system and pals: A peer-mediated augmentative and alternative communication intervention for minimally verbal preschoolers with autism. Journal of Speech, Language, and Hearing Research, 59(5), 1133-1145.

Tiger, J.H., Hanley, G.P., Bruzek, J. (2008). Functional communication training: a review and practical guide. Behavior Analysis in Practice, 1(1), 16-23.

van der Meer, L., Sutherland, D., O'Reilly, M. F., Lancioni, G. E., & Sigafoos, J. (2012). A further comparison of manual signing, picture exchange, and speech-generating devices as communication modes for children with autism spectrum disorders. Research in Autism Spectrum Disorders, 6(4), 1247–1257. Elsevier BV.

Walker, V. L., Carpenter, M. E., Clausen, A., Ealer, K., & Lyon, K. J. (2020). Special educators as coaches to support paraprofessional implementation of functional communication training. Journal of Positive Behavior Interventions.

Wendt, O., Hsu, N., Simon, K., Dienhart, A., & Cain, L. (2019). Effects of an iPad-based speech-generating device infused into instruction with the picture exchange communication system for adolescents and

The Power
of *Visuals*

Visuals have long been known to amplify understanding, retention, and engagement when learning new skills. Within the fields of Applied Behavior Analysis (ABA) and Special Education, the positive influence of using visuals to support learners is widely accepted and celebrated. Visual supports have become indispensable tools in homes and classrooms. Yet, there's a noticeable gap in leveraging visual teaching when it comes to supporting parents, educators, and behavior support staff.

ABA Visualized is proud to be the first to take an innovative approach to teaching evidence-based behavior strategies through step-by-step visuals, making complex information more approachable, accessible, and relatable. Inspired by the many stories shared about the positive impact of visuals in behavior support, we are taking this work one step further by creating an online platform that makes behavior expertise accessible through visuals. BIP Visualized allows behavior professionals to create and customize their own visual behavior plans, access a growing library of visual strategies, resources, and on-demand trainings developed in collaboration with autistic consultants, and share everything directly with families, teachers, and behavior staff. This is the only platform built to support behavior planning, learning, and collaboration entirely through visuals.

With any of our new products, first comes a research deep dive to fully understand current barriers and experiences. In the following infographic, we're highlighting research findings comparing text-based learning with visual learning. We explore established multidisciplinary research on the efficacy of visuals versus text and reveal insights specific to the field of ABA. We've also been busy collecting our own research! With the recognized success of ABA Visualized's signature visual teaching style, we have been testing the impact of applying this approach to developing and disseminating Behavior Intervention Plans (BIPs). We're finding that teaching families and educators through text leads to low buy-in, low engagement, low understanding, and most importantly, low impact on the learner. Further, in our survey of over 200 behavior experts, only 35% reported feeling effective with their current teaching approach. Instead, when behavior strategies are taught through visuals, families and educators are more engaged, have better understanding, remember the skills longer, implement it more accurately, and feel more confident!

We're excited to share some of these findings with you, some of which may be eye-opening when considering their implications for the quality of services and care provided to our learners and their stakeholders. Our hope is that by highlighting the power of visuals, you will feel inspired to become a visual storyteller yourself!

Teaching with Text
The Traditional Way

Low Understanding

Text often leads to low understanding, which hinders parents' ability to advocate for their child's needs and potentially causes misinterpretation of recommended strategies.

(Banks et al., 2018; Critchfield et al., 2017)

Low Acceptance

The use of technical language in behavior recommendations can lead to reduced acceptance of the recommendations, particularly among individuals with little or no training in ABA principles. In fact, researchers found that people rate ABA jargon as "not motivating" and "unpleasant."

(Banks et al., 2018; Critchfield et al., 2017)

Low Engagement

Teaching through complex text can lead to low engagement because the team may struggle to follow behavior recommendations and resist change when the language is overly technical or hard to understand.

(Banks et al., 2018; Critchfield et al., 2017)

Low Accessibility

Text is not always accessible to everyone, as language barriers, especially for families with limited English proficiency, can hinder understanding and communication during behavior intervention discussions, leading to reduced parental engagement, misunderstandings, and increased stress and anxiety related to their child's needs.

(Andrade, Hancock, & Whaley, 2019; Bradshaw & Richey, 2015; Hatcher et al., 2016, Taylor & Landrum, 2016).

Low Confidence

Complex technical behavior recommendations can lead to low confidence as they often result in confusion, stress, and ineffective implementation, leaving stakeholders feeling unsupported and service providers ineffective.

In our own survey of people responsible for implementing behavior strategies, only 40% reported feeling confident and only 28% reported feeling prepared.

Feeling confident in using strategies

40%

Feeling prepared to support behaviors

28%

(Banks et al., 2018; Holt et al., 2016; Jarmolowicz et al., 2008; McMahon, Feldberg, & Ardoin, 2021).

Low Accuracy

Research shows that typical teaching approaches result in low accuracy with team members implementing less than 60% of the recommended strategies, and those being done so with an average accuracy rate of only 68%.

Parents & teachers report struggling to understand and implement complex technical instructions effectively.

Strategies implemented

60%

Accuracy of implemented strategies

68%

(de Bruin et al., 2014; Scheibel et al., 2022; Walker et al., 2021)

Low Collaboration

The use of technical language in behavior strategies often creates communication barriers, hindering effective collaboration between behavior specialists and stakeholders like parents and teachers.

In our own survey, only 25% of people responsible for implementing behavior strategies reported being aware of what strategies were being used in other settings.

(Peterson et al., 2018; Sailor & McCarthy, 2015)

Difficult to Remember

Text is easy to forget because our brain quickly loses information, we often overlook the middle parts of long texts, and dense material can overwhelm us.

In our pilot study, we found the average number of strategies included in a BIP was 26. However, the average number of strategies a person responsible for implementing could recall was only 3.

(The Forgetting Curve, Serial Position Effect, Cognitive Load Theory)

The Forgetting Curve for Text

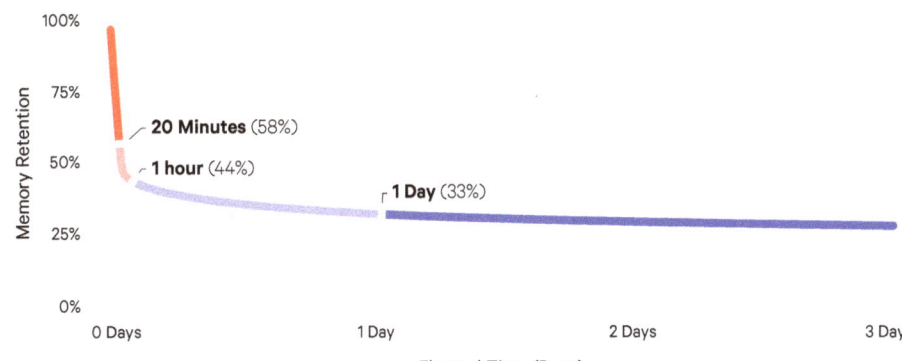

20 Minutes (58%)

1 hour (44%)

1 Day (33%)

Memory Retention

Elapsed Time (Days)

Teaching with Images
Our Innovative Approach

Better Understanding

Visuals make concepts easier to understand and they help teachers and parents better grasp behavior management strategies, making learning and skill application more effective.

(Albers & Greer, 2010; Eberhard, K., 2021; Hughes & Frederick, 2006; Sung-Hee, K., 2022).

More Preferred

Research has shown that most people overwhelmingly prefer and find instructions with visuals easier to use than traditional written instructions, indicating a clear preference for visuals over text-based content.

(Graff & Karsten, 2012).

More Engagement

Visuals improve engagement by capturing and holding the viewer's attention more effectively, as shown through eye-tracking studies. Visual storytelling makes the content more memorable and viewers engage longer.

(Harsh et al., 2019; HubSpot, 2022; Paradi, D., 1986).

More Accessible for Diverse Needs

Visuals offer greater accessibility, ensuring that those with diverse needs can access and understand the information.

(Abdulrahaman, et al., 2020).

Increased Confidence

Training with visual supports has been shown to boost confidence among parents and teachers in managing challenging behaviors.

(Clees & Brady, 2006).

Better Collaboration

The use of visuals has been shown to enhance communication between service providers, parents, teachers, fostering more effective collaboration in behavior management.

(Zarcone & Lindauer, 2006).

Higher Accuracy

Visuals significantly improve accuracy in comprehension, recall, and implementation. In one study, participants' accuracy in a behavior skill went from 38% to 99% when diagrams were added to the instructions, and accurate learning took less time!

Accuracy when taught with text

  38%

Accuracy when taught with visuals

 99%

Additionally, visual supports have been shown to improve educators' accuracy of implementing behavior strategies in both special education and general education classroom settings.

(Arco & Ricci, 2018; Graff & Karsten, 2012; Koegel & Koegel, 2006; Meyer & Bohning, 2011)

Better Retention

Using visuals alongside words makes information easier to remember because it engages different parts of the brain, reduces mental effort, and helps people see and remember relationships and patterns, ultimately improving retention.

Research has shown that people tend to remember information with visuals significantly better than text alone (65% compared to 10%), which is widely understood as "the picture superiority effect."

Remembering textual content

  10%

Remembering visual content

 65%

In our own pilot study, accurate recall improved by 57% when behavior strategies were presented as visuals instead of text.

(Dual Coding Theory, The Picture Superiority Effect, Cognitive Load Theory).

BIP Visualized

BIP Visualized is an online platform that makes behavior expertise more accessible through visuals. It supports behavior professionals in creating and customizing visual Behavior Intervention Plans while also providing a growing library of visual strategies, resources, and on demand trainings developed in collaboration with autistic consultants. All materials are designed to be shared directly with families, educators, and behavior staff.

While BIPs are well supported by research, many providers report challenges when plans are long, technical, or difficult for teams to understand and implement consistently. BIP Visualized replaces traditional text heavy approaches with step by step visual tools that are easier to learn, teach, and apply across settings. This visual approach supports clearer communication, stronger follow through, and more consistent support for learners at home, in schools, and in the community.

Try it out at **BIPVisualized.com**

"As a seasoned BCBA, I can confidently say that BIP Visualized is a game-changer for the field of Applied Behavior Analysis"

Steven Camp, CEO at CAMP

"Please make this part of your toolbox of resources, you will not be disappointed!"

Shayla, School Psychologist at Fresno USD

"BIP Visualized is AMAZING!!! It's a lifesaver for BCBAs, a visual map for families, and filled with strategies everyone can use immediately."

Julia Bernasconi, BCBA

How a Visual Behavior Plan Works

Mova Tantrums

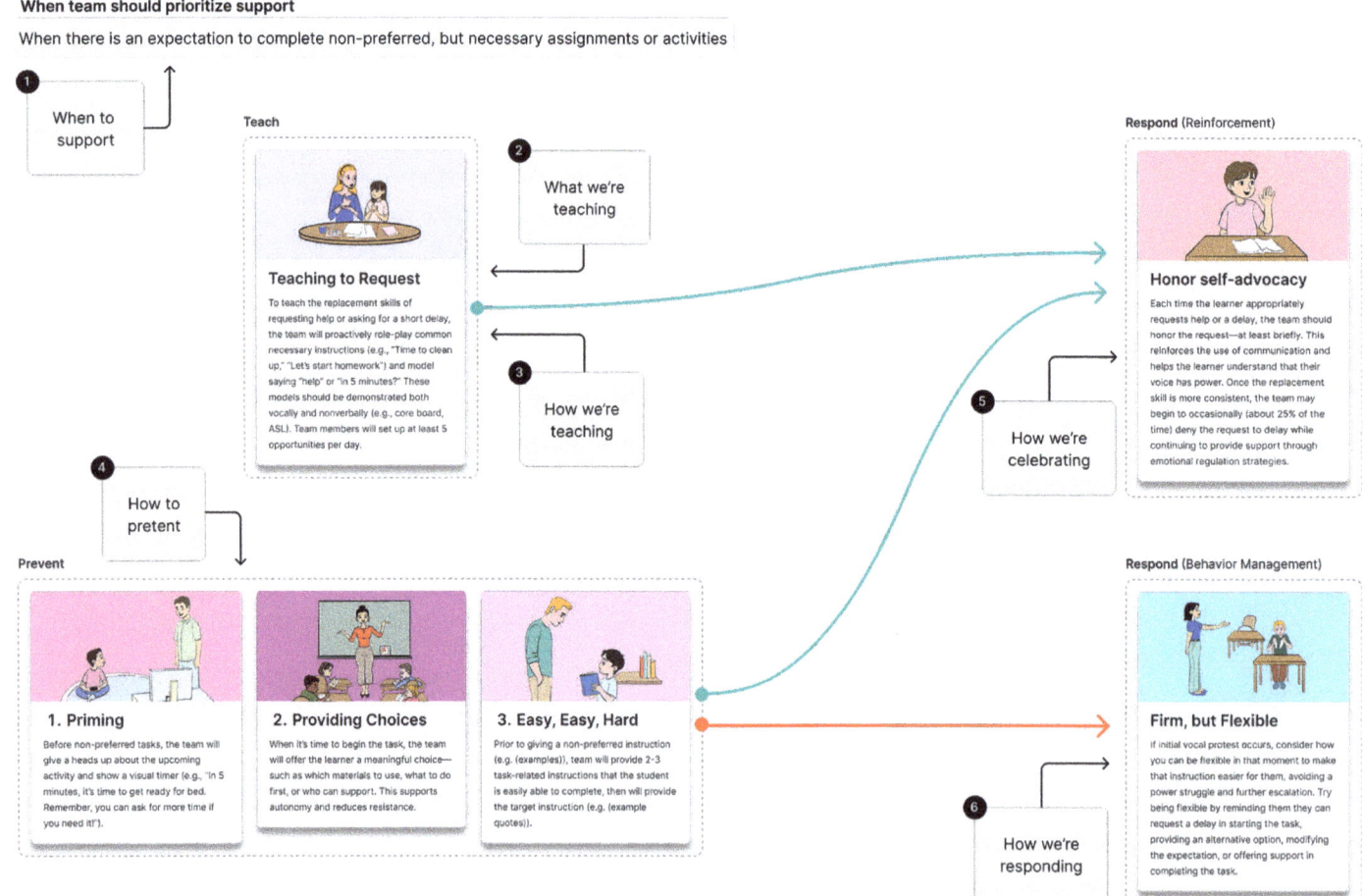

What Makes Us Different

Save time without sacrificing quality

Clear step-by-step visuals

Focus on practical real-life applications

Neurodiversity-affirming

Unlimited sharing

Trainings for the whole team

What You Can Do with BIP Visualized

Create Your Own Visual BIP

Go to "Create a visual BIP" and simply drag and drop evidence-based strategies to build a visual step-by-step plan for your team!

Features
~ Easy fill-in-the-blank descriptions
~ Fully customizable strategies
~ Print, download, or share
~ Real-time co-editing

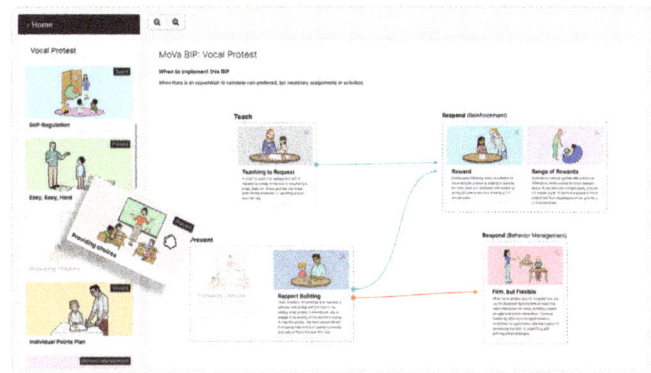

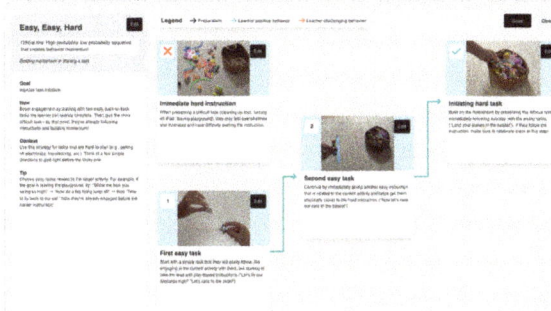

Edit and Customize Strategies

Edit strategies with your own images and text to make them completely individualized. Just click "Edit" on the top right of any strategy to customize!

Features
~ Upload images
~ Edit text
~ Save as template to reuse

Explore Courses and Resources to Share

Access a growing collection of trainings and resources to expand your own clinical expertise & support your team between sessions! Your account includes unlimited sharing, so your team can access everything you share—completely free.

We have trainings for
~ CEU trainings for BCBAs
~ Shareable trainings for educators
~ Shareable training for families

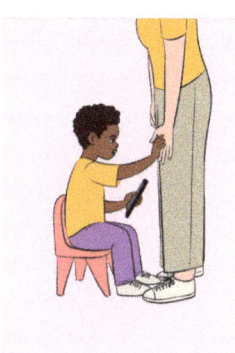